# Hazel Larsen Archer

## Black Mountain College Photographer

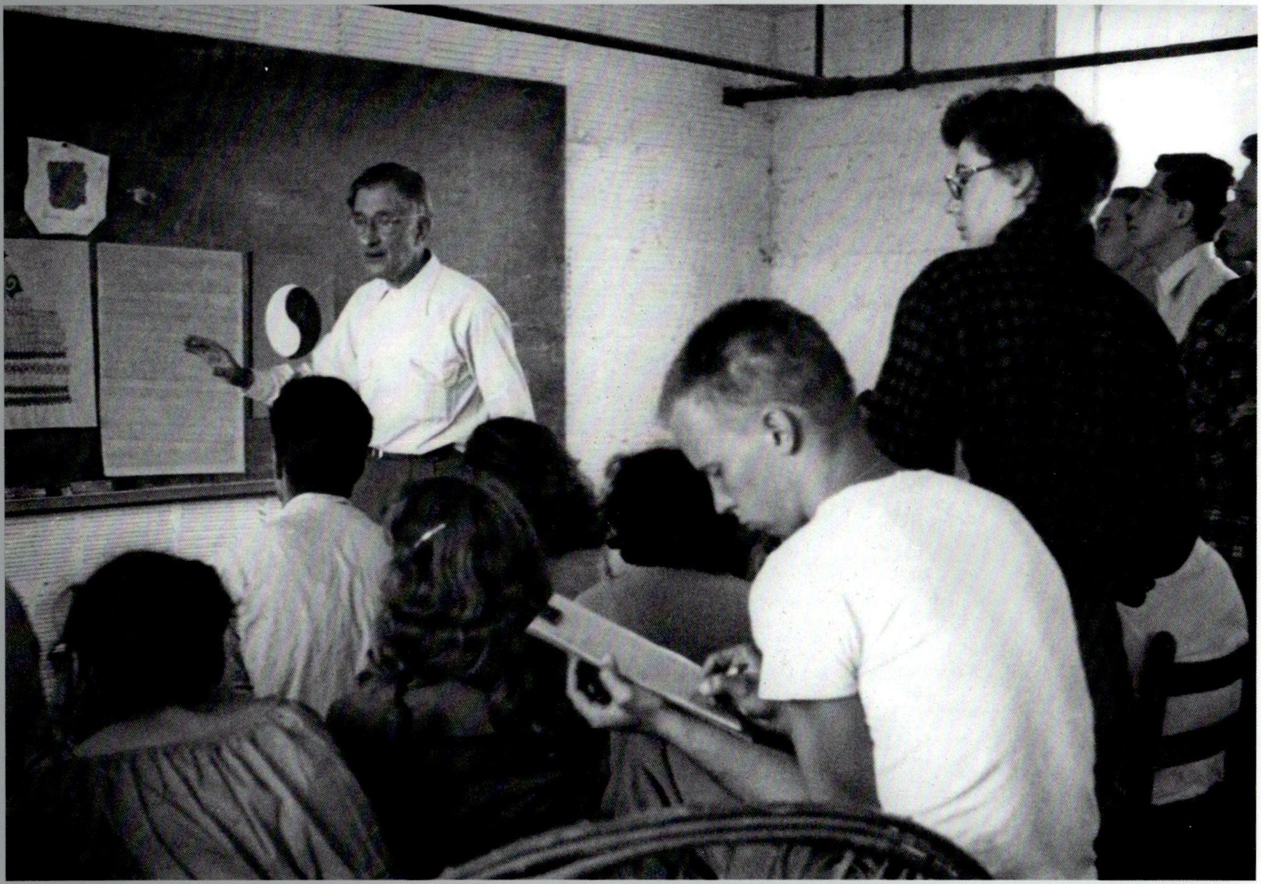

Black Mountain College
MUSEUM + ARTS CENTER

Black Mountain College
**MUSEUM + ARTS CENTER**

P.O. Box 18912
Asheville, NC 28814

www.blackmountaincollege.org
bmcmac@bellsouth.net

LARGE COVER PHOTOGRAPH
The path from the Dining Hall to the Studies Building

PREVIOUS PAGE PHOTOGRAPH
Josef Albers lecturing with Ray Johnson in the foreground



ISBN 0-9774138-0-2

This book is published in conjunction with the exhibition
**Hazel Larsen Archer: Black Mountain College Photographer**

April 21 – August 12, 2006
Black Mountain College Museum + Arts Center
56 Broadway
Asheville, North Carolina

August 22 – September 23, 2006
Fine Art Museum
at the Fine & Performing Arts Center
Western Carolina University
Cullowhee, North Carolina

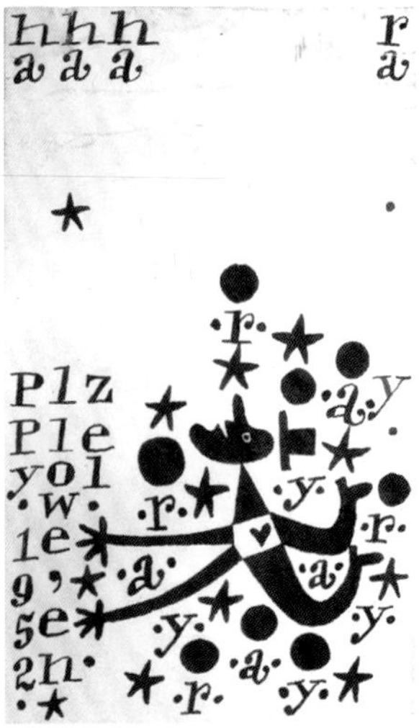

"Happy Halloween" Card
to Hazel from Ray Johnson, 1952

North Carolina arts Council
www.ncarts.org

This project received support from the North Carolina Arts Council, an agency funded by the State of North Carolina and the National Endowment for the Arts, which believes that a great nation deserves great art.

This publication has been made possible through the generous support of the following: Asheville Savings Bank, John E. Cram, Joe and Cynthia Kimmel, Joscelyn W. Hill, North Carolina Arts Council, Western Carolina University Fine Art Museum, Rob Pulleyn, Mary Holden Thompson, f/32 Photo Group, and Jack and Helga Beam.

**COLOPHON**

PRINTING
Blue Ridge Printing
Asheville, NC

PRESS
Komori L640, 40" Six Color

PAPER
StoraEnso
Gusto Satin 100# Text
Gusto Satin 100# Cover

FONTS
Univers 47, 57 and 67
Goudy

DESIGN
Susan Rhew Design Inc.
Asheville, NC

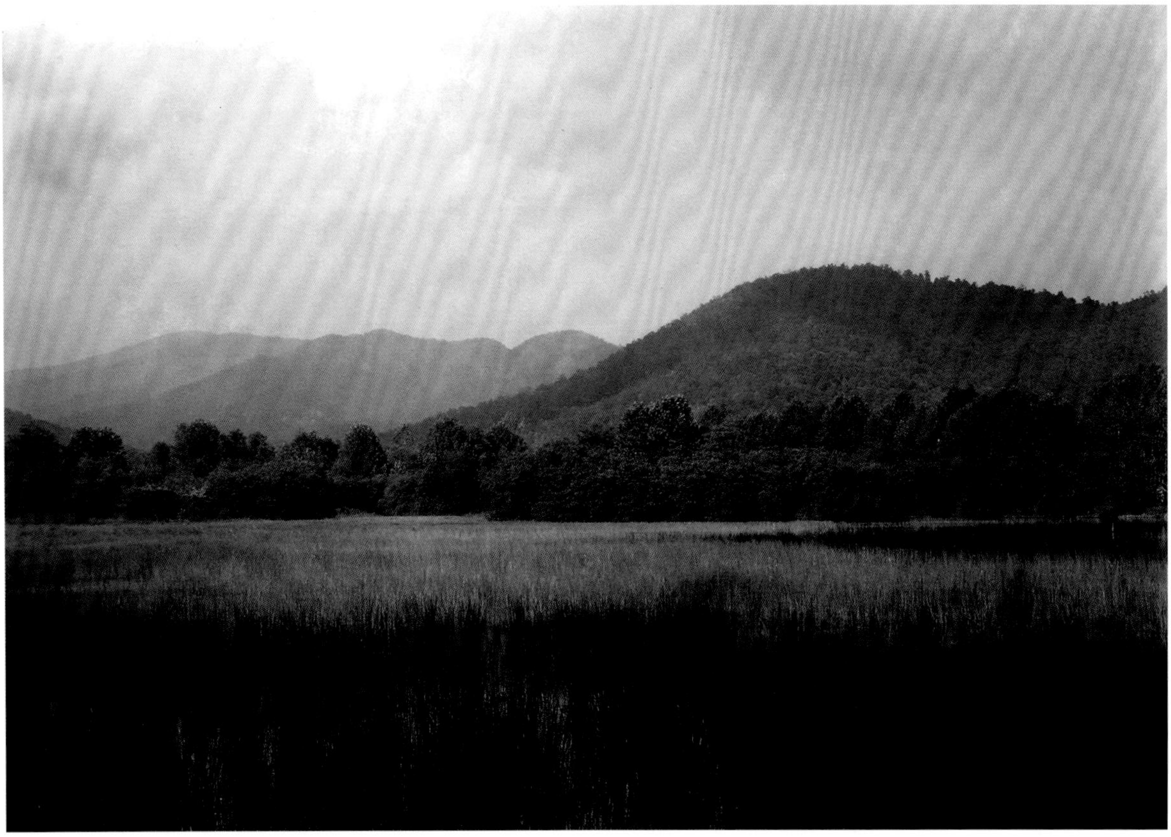

View of mountains beyond Lake Eden

# TABLE OF CONTENTS


ACKNOWLEDGMENTS 5
JOHN WRIGHT / ALICE SEBRELL

BLACK MOUNTAIN COLLEGE: A RARE PLACE 6
CONNIE BOSTIC

MOTION STUDIES 9
DAVID VAUGHAN

CAPTURING LIGHT 18
ERIKA ZAROW

PLATES 20

GUGGENHEIM FELLOWSHIP LETTER OF RECOMMENDATION 90
R. BUCKMINSTER FULLER

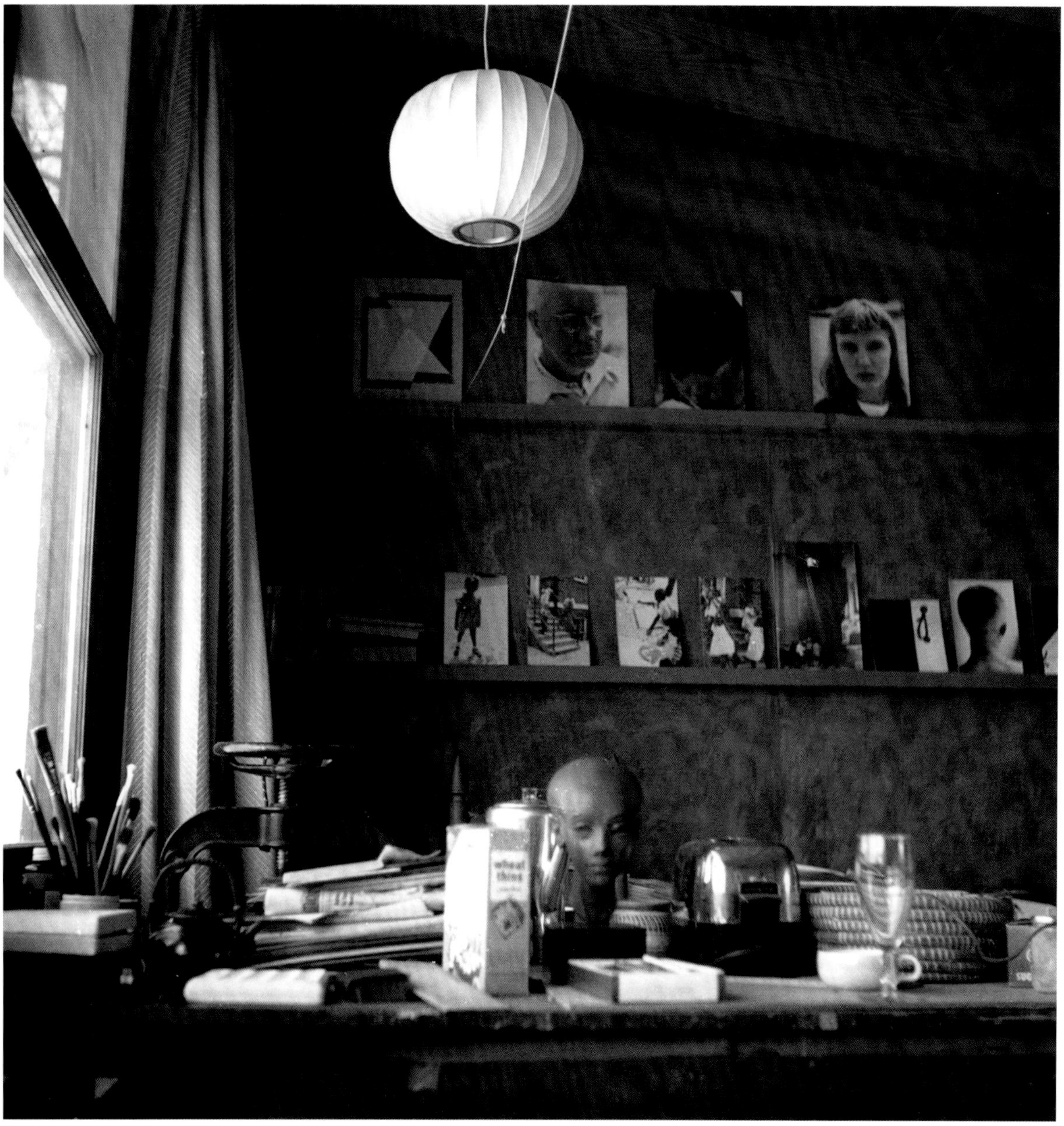

Archer's desk

# ACKNOWLEDGMENTS

For those of us involved with the Black Mountain College Museum + Arts Center it is a great pleasure to bring the extraordinary photographs made by Hazel Larsen Archer at Black Mountain College into book form. Archer's photographs of the people, the landscape, the community that was BMC in the mid-to-late 1940s and early 1950s are, quite simply, wonderful. She had a way with portraiture, certainly, but her attention to the landscape is noteworthy as well. The doors of the Quiet House were observed and photographed with such dedication and respect that one would think them a holy relic. It is clear that Hazel had a passion for Black Mountain College. Her photographs are the remnants of a nine-year love affair with a unique community of creative, eccentric, sometimes difficult, always complicated individuals. The place was aptly named Lake Eden.

Hazel Larsen Archer was a polio survivor. She traveled by wheelchair, but it did not seem to limit her much, if at all. One senses her intensity — and her sensitivity — just looking at the images. The mere inability to walk would not deter this woman. Such determination and talent were present in many of those who found their way to Black Mountain College. How else can we explain the enormous impact that BMC faculty and alumni have had — and continue to have — on our world? This book is dedicated to all of those who were there and who have shared their bounty with those of us who weren't there — but wish we had been.

A few very important individuals have helped move this book from idea to reality. The Board of Directors of the Black Mountain College Museum + Arts Center have been supportive throughout. Special thanks go to Board Members John E. Cram and Connie Bostic for contributions too numerous to list, to Mary Holden Thompson for crucial logistical support in Paris, and to Susan Rhew for designing a beautiful book. Thanks to David Vaughan, archivist for the Cunningham Dance Company, for his lovely essay entitled ***Motion Studies*** and to Erika Zarow, Archer's daughter, for her extraordinary memoir of time spent as a child in the company of her mother. To Martin DeWitt, Director of the Fine Art Museum at Western Carolina University, we extend our thanks for hosting the exhibition on the second leg of its journey and to Audrey Veres our deep appreciation for her superb assistance when called upon. Of course, without financial support this book would never have happened, and so, with enormous gratitude, we acknowledge the following donors: Asheville Savings Bank, John E. Cram, Joe and Cynthia Kimmel, Joscelyn W. Hill, North Carolina Arts Council, Western Carolina University Fine Art Museum, Rob Pulleyn, Mary Holden Thompson, f/32 Photo Group, and Jack and Helga Beam.

Additional thanks go to Erika Zarow and to Jan van der Donk for making Archer's prints and negatives available to us for this book and the exhibition that accompanies it. We hope we have done justice to the material you entrusted to our care. Thanks also to Michael Harrison for additional assistance in this regard. Whenever possible we have tried to identify the subjects of portraits, but there are a few who remain unknown — to us. Our profound appreciation goes to Mary Emma Harris for her help in providing names for some of the individuals who sat in front of Archer's camera. To BMC faculty and alumni Merce Cunningham, Joan Heller, Merrill Gillespie, Dorothea Rockburne, Michael Rumaker, Marie Stilkind, Vera Baker Williams, and Jonathan Williams thank you for your help with this project and for your role in carrying the flame into the 21st century.

JOHN WRIGHT, BOARD CHAIR, BLACK MOUNTAIN COLLEGE MUSEUM + ARTS CENTER
ALICE SEBRELL, PROJECT COORDINATOR, BLACK MOUNTAIN COLLEGE MUSEUM + ARTS CENTER

# BLACK MOUNTAIN COLLEGE: A RARE PLACE

BY CONNIE BOSTIC

In 1933 Franklin Roosevelt became president of an America devastated by the 1929 stock market crash. The unemployment rate was 25%. Farm income was down 50%. Bread lines were common, and displaced families wandered the nation's roads searching for food and shelter. It was in this year and this milieu that Black Mountain College was founded.

It must have taken a great deal of courage for the little band of dedicated teachers, outraged at the firing of a colleague, to uproot their families with the idea of forming a new college in one summer. The tone for the school was set when its founder, John Andrew Rice, said, "If I can't get the right man for art, the thing won't work." He got the right man: he hired Josef Albers, who had left Germany because Hitler had closed the Bauhaus where he had been teaching and because his wife, the weaver and designer Anni Albers, was Jewish. Albers spoke not one word of English when he arrived and taught at Black Mountain for sixteen years, influencing not only his students there, but ultimately the whole of mid-twentieth century art.

Black Mountain College, however, was not an art school. It was a liberal arts college with classes in languages, the sciences, mathematics, and philosophy. Rice was a classics scholar, but his ideas about learning went beyond the systems of education in the traditional academic world, both then and now. Rice's influence on education, and that of Albers and many of the other teachers at Black Mountain, has had national and indeed international implications. It was Rice's belief that to understand music, a student did not just listen to a symphony: he learned to play an instrument. To learn the history of art he made a painting, and to appreciate theatre he acted in a play. This led to interdisciplinary experiences which enriched the lives of the students by making them aware of the potential for deep understanding and a life of exploration and discovery.

The teachers and their families lived with the students on the campus. They shared meals in the college dining room and danced together on Saturday nights. If an interesting discussion started in a class it was frequently continued in the dining hall, joined by students not in the class, and carried on into the night or even into the next day. Black Mountain students were not given grades. When the college felt that a student had finished his or her studies, outside examiners were brought in to verify the student's accomplishments. Graduate programs all over the country accepted Black Mountain students who had no formal diploma.

When the United States entered World War II many of the young men at Black Mountain College volunteered for military service or were drafted. At the end of the war there was an influx of students who could afford to pay tuition because of the G.I. Bill. Among these was Asheville native Kenneth Noland and two of his brothers and a young Texan named Robert Rauschenberg.

When polio survivor Hazel Larsen arrived in her wheelchair for the Summer Institute in 1944 Black Mountain College was host to artists in many disciplines who would later become world famous. Not only do her photographs inspire awe for their insight and beauty, they provide an invaluable record of a time and a place that changed our culture. The photographs are for the most part undated, untitled, and without any identification. We are left with the record of an era: no specifics. It has to be enough.

A 1948 fire in the chemistry lab/darkroom (purportedly started by college tutor Madame Goldowski's vodka still) destroyed many of Larsen's negatives, but she continued her work, photographing not only her friends, but also her surroundings. The bucolic setting of the school may have been

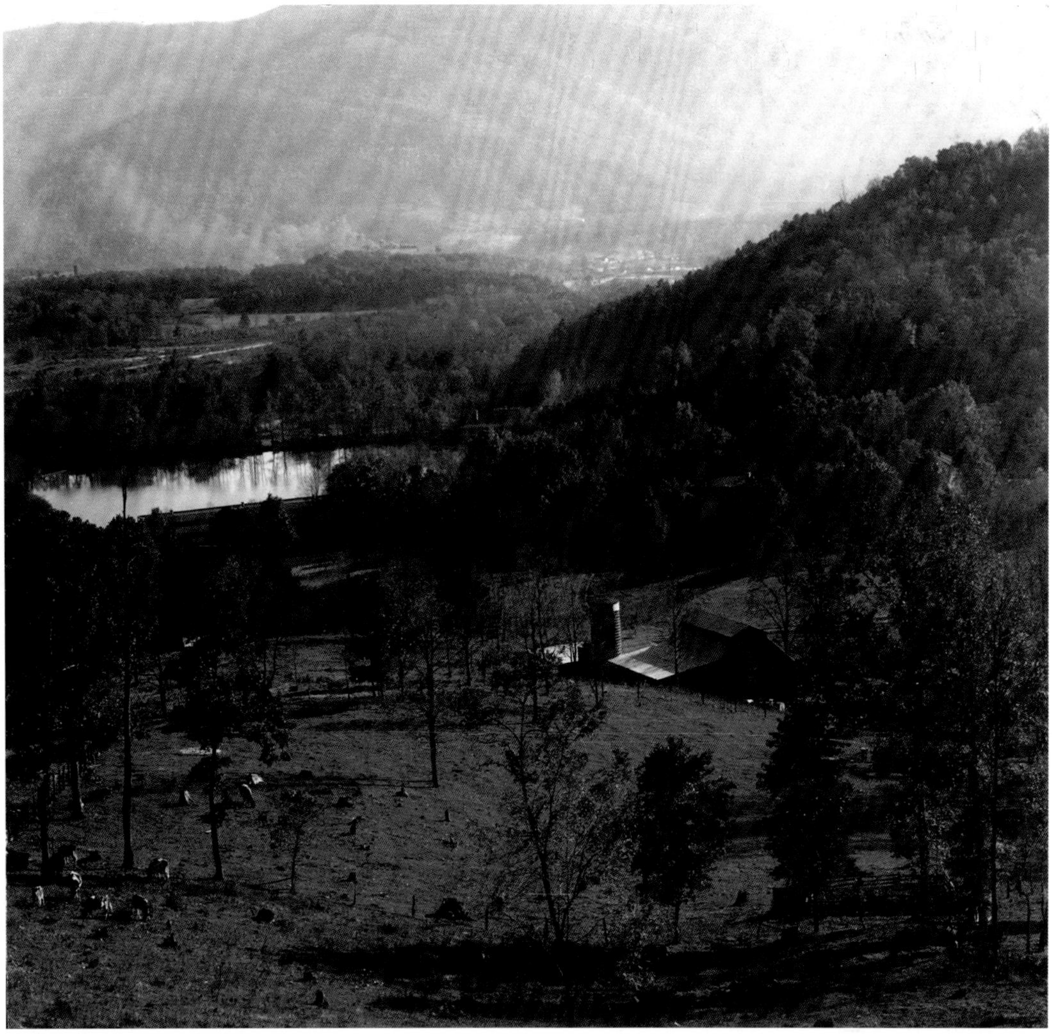

View of Black Mountain College campus at Lake Eden

best described upon his arrival at the school by literature teacher Edward Dahlberg: "...a rare place...for tender human beings...to come for the living waters." However, just before his departure two weeks later he referred to the same landscape as having trees that were "...savage, serpentine."

Dahlberg's stormy two weeks at Black Mountain gives an extreme example of the sometimes highly charged atmosphere at the college. Many of the brilliant teachers and students at the school were strong-minded and opinionated: conflicts arose around many topics, those having to do with education and those having to do with the personal lives of the members of the community. The beauty of the lake or the comforting enclosing presence of the mountains seems to have done little to resolve these disturbances.

Things changed at the school after the departure of Josef and Anni Albers in 1949. By 1951 when the poet Charles Olson became rector there was less emphasis on a liberal arts curriculum. Black Mountain was becoming a center for new American writing. Many of the alumni from the earlier days of the college deplored the changes, but out of these changes came a renewed energy in literature that helped to define much of the post-World War II generation. By the time Hazel Larsen Archer left the college in 1953 it was clear that the end was near. Enrollment was low, and money worries which had plagued the college from the start reached a new high. We are grateful to have Larsen's record of this seminal time in the cultural history of our region, our state and our nation.

Connie Bostic is a painter, writer and board member of the Black Mountain College Museum + Arts Center.

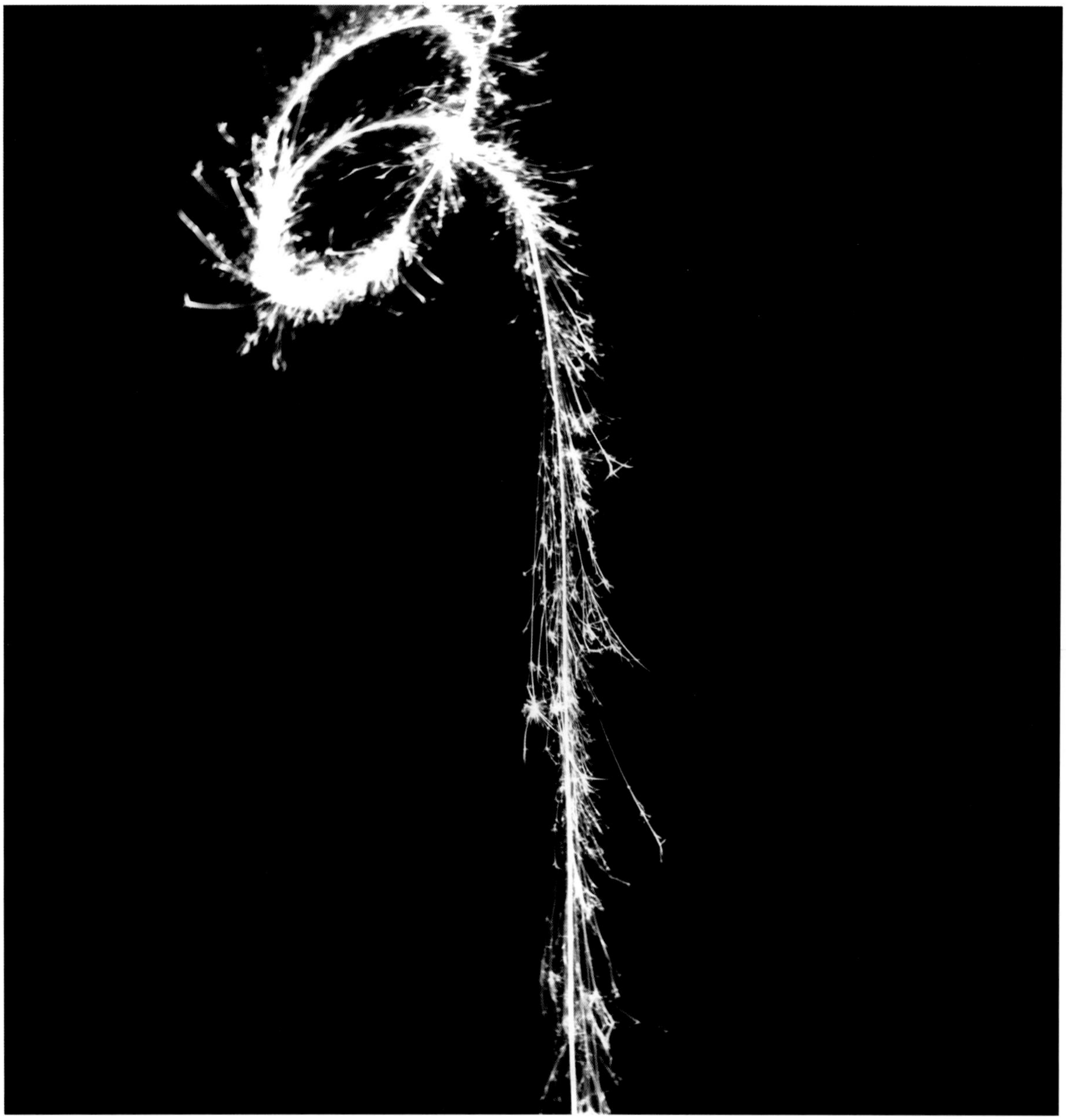

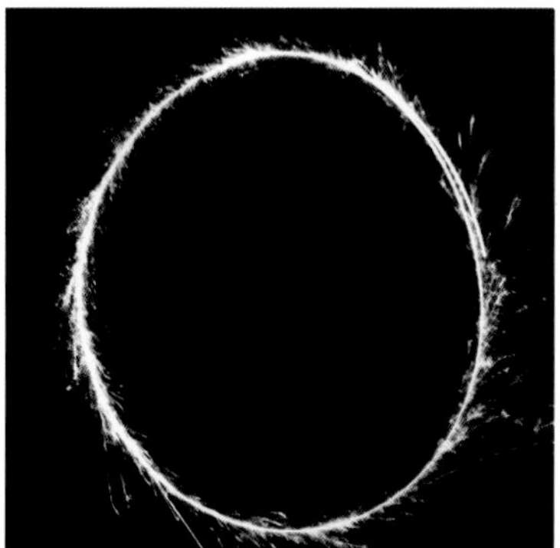

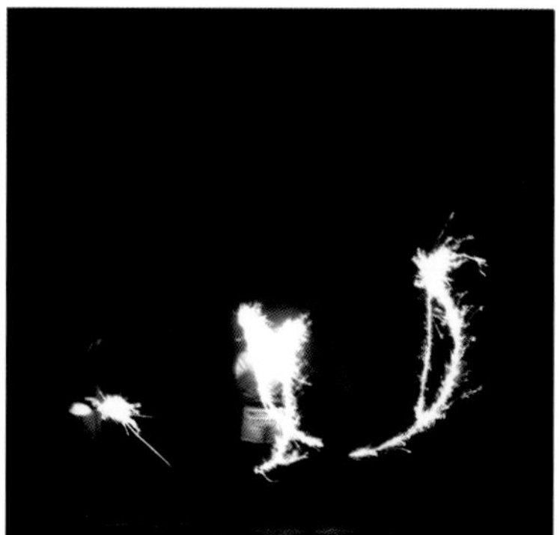

Untitled

# MOTION STUDIES

BY DAVID VAUGHAN

The importance of Black Mountain College, the progressive liberal arts school in North Carolina, in the history of the arts in America in the twentieth century is out of all proportion to the length of its existence. Opening as a pioneering experiment in education in the fall of 1933, the college soon became a hotbed of avant-garde activity in all the fine and performing arts. By the fall of 1956 the experiment had run its course, most of the faculty had quit, and those who remained decided to close the school. But its ideas and values were kept alive by those who taught and studied there, and Black Mountain has remained a symbol of experimental energy and artistic idealism.

The photographer Hazel-Frieda Larsen first went to the college as a student in the summer of 1944. She had been one of a group of art students at Milwaukee State Teachers' College that included W.P. (Pete) and Elizabeth (Betty) Jennerjahn. Betty was the first to go to Black Mountain, and was so enthusiastic about her experience there — and in particular about studying with Josef Albers — that the others soon followed. Albers had left Germany for the United States in November 1933, soon after the Nazis came into power and shut down the Bauhaus, where he had taught. He was at once invited to the recently established Black Mountain College and appointed Professor of Art, initially for one year. He remained for sixteen years, together with his wife Anni, both of them influential teachers. Other immigrants from Germany followed, Walter Gropius and Lyonel Feininger among them. As Mary Emma Harris writes in her 1987 history ***The Arts at Black Mountain College***, "Black Mountain was in many respects the spiritual heir to the Bauhaus. They shared a common experimental and anti-academic spirit, a belief in the social responsibility of education and the arts, and an organization that involved both faculty and students in the decision-making process."[1]

Larsen returned in 1945 to do graduate work with Albers. She also studied at the college with Buckminster Fuller, Lyonel Feininger, Willem de Kooning, and Robert Motherwell; Walter Gropius; the photographers Beaumont and Nancy Newhall; and the graphic designers Leo Lionni and Alvin Lustig —a list of names that is indicative of the kind of charismatic teachers who were drawn to the school.[2] Both Larsen and the Jennerjahns later joined the Black Mountain faculty; Larsen was appointed the school's first full-time teacher of photography in 1949. This was no doubt in recognition of the work she had done at the school, particularly in the previous summer.

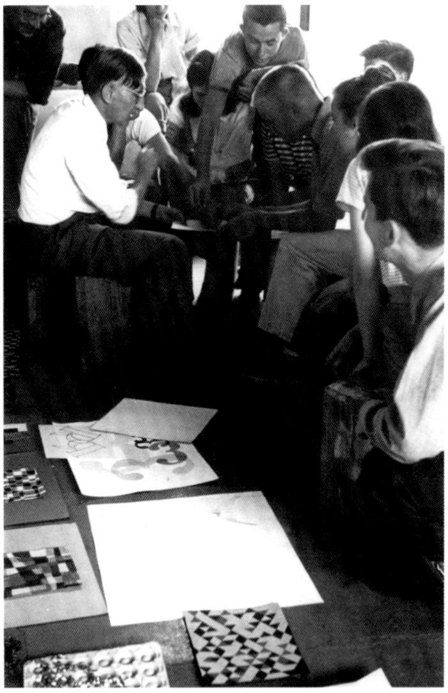

Josef Albers teaching design

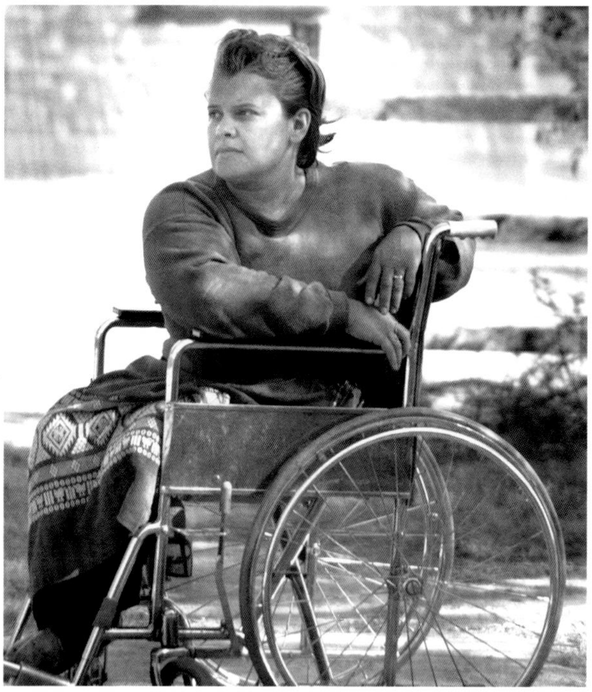

Hazel Larsen Archer

That summer, 1948, was remarkable, even for Black Mountain, for the extraordinary array of creative talent in both faculty and students. As Harris observes, the summer "marked the end of the dominance of the European artists at the college and the emergence of the young Americans, who were to be the creative leaders in the arts in the United States for the next twenty-five years"[3]: John Cage taught music; Merce Cunningham dance; Buckminster Fuller architecture. Willem and Elaine de Kooning were invited at Cage's suggestion. (Although de Kooning had recently had his first one-man show at the Egan Gallery in New York, they were glad to go because they had been evicted from their apartment.) Richard Lippold was sculptor in residence; his wife, the dancer Louise Lippold was with him and studied with Cunningham. Ray Johnson and Arthur Penn were among the students.

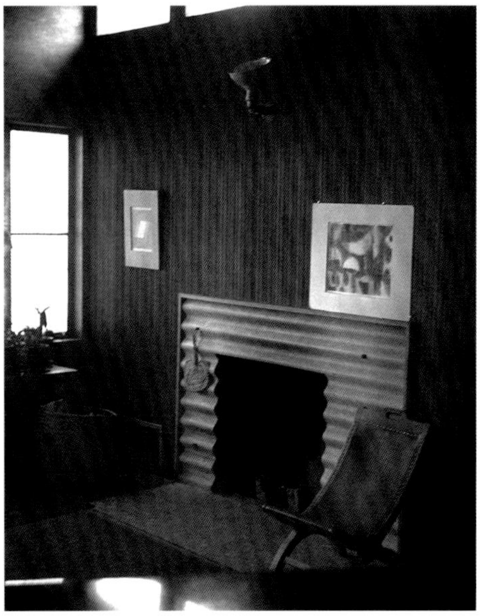

Interior of the Jalowetz Cottage

Cage put on a festival of the music of Erik Satie culminating in a performance of the composer's play ***Le Piège de Méduse***, translated by the poet Mary Caroline Richards, who was on the college faculty, as ***The Ruse of Medusa***. Fuller played the Baron Medusa, Elaine de Kooning his daughter. Arthur Penn co-directed the show with Helen Livingston. The de Koonings designed the décor. Cunningham appeared as "Jonas, a costly mechanical monkey," and choreographed his own dances, which he performed as a separate number in a concert he gave later in the summer with Louise Lippold and other dance students. The monkey's tail was by Richard Lippold.

Larsen, for her part, made an extraordinary series of images of Cunningham dancing, in the open air on the grounds of the college. The photographs seem to depict two sequences of movement, perhaps taken on different days: one in which Cunningham is wearing black pants and sweater, the

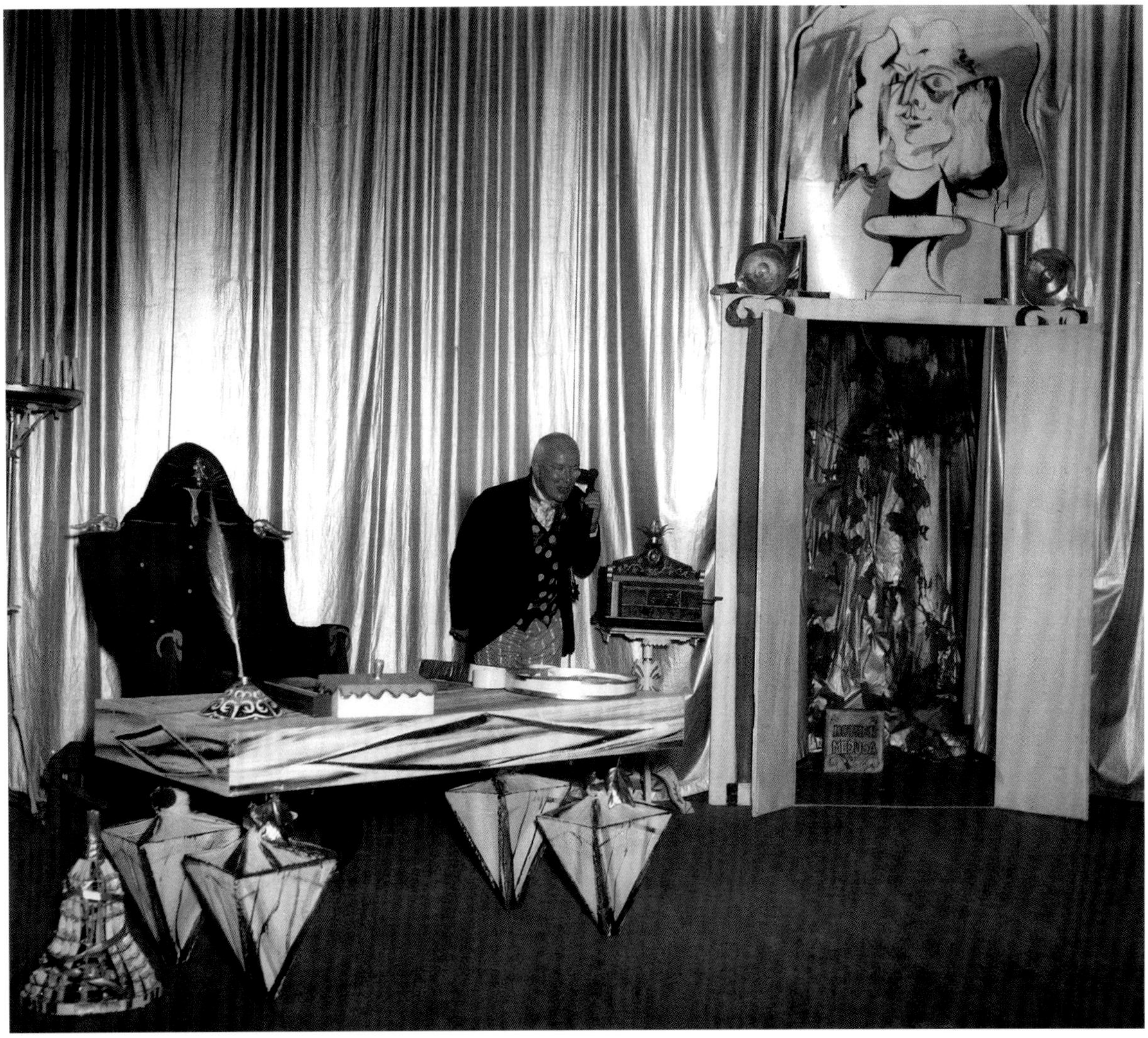

Buckminster Fuller as the Baron Medusa in "The Ruse of Medusa," Summer 1948. The set was designed by Willem and Elaine de Kooning

other in which he wears gray pants and a white shirt. He improvised movement as she took the pictures: he remembers that it was difficult because Larsen was very close to him — she was a victim of polio and was confined to a wheelchair, so that she remained stationary while he moved.

The images are notable for their absolute clarity — although there is no retouching — they are almost like frames from a film. Some photographers try to give a sense of movement by blurring the image, but this is not how the eye perceives dance movement, unless it is very fast. Larsen's images give the sense of a dance phrase when framed in series of three or four. Singly they have a certain abstract quality due to the way Larsen cropped them, often cutting off Cunningham's head or extremities. In these pictures the negative space is as important as the shape of his body — as is true of Cunningham's dances. This is particularly noticeable in the black series, where his figure is silhouetted against the background of trees. Larsen was in the habit of writing "Do not trim or crop this photograph" on the back of her prints, so that there would be no attempt to "correct" or improve the way she had cropped them herself. According to Andrew Oates, one of her students, her practice of cropping images was done in the camera itself, and she encouraged her students to do the same: "She always wanted to use the full negative when printing a photograph, and encouraged us to design an image when looking through the camera lens."[4]

Larsen also made portraits of Cunningham, Cage, Johnson, and others who were present that summer. The portrait series of Cunningham was made with Larsen again very close and having him turn around while she clicked the shutter, so that his head is seen in close-up from front, side, and back. (She seems to have photographed both Cage and Johnson in the same way.) Her other sitters included Josef and Anni Albers, Ruth Asawa, the de Koonings, Fuller, Charles Olson, Dorothea Rockburne, and (later) Robert Rauschenberg and his wife Sue Weil. Another dance subject shows Rauschenberg dancing with Betty Jennerjahn, who studied with Cunningham in the summer of 1948 and later became a dance instructor at the college. (Rauschenberg took her class; she remembers spending hours "one-on-one" with him.) Pete Jennerjahn has said that Larsen was "maddeningly deliberate" in her methods, whether loading new film in her camera or "getting it set up to get the right angle."[5]

The abstract quality seen in her dance pictures is apparent in other photographs she made in and around Black Mountain — images of trees, leaves, grass, the doors of the "Quiet House" at the College (a small building for meditation), a nearby Baptist church and its graveyard. There are also "Sunprints," her photographic version of the studies that all students made in Albers's course in basic design, which he called ***Werklehre*** (loosely, "craft studies"). In her own classes, Larsen taught "in the areas of painting, photography, color, basic design, drawing, history of photography."[6] (Pete Jennerjahn remembers her talking in class about the work of Julia Margaret Cameron.)

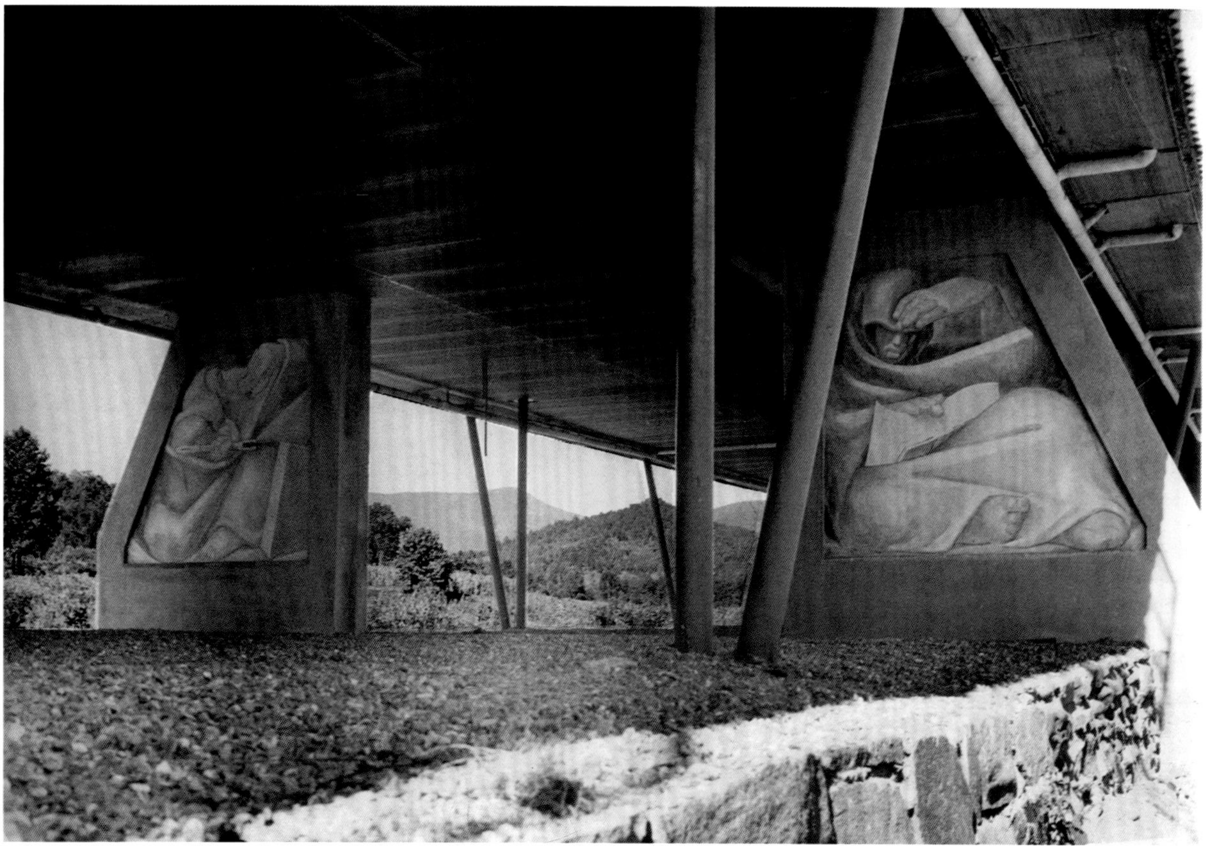

Fresco murals by Jean Charlot underneath the Studies Building — *Inspiration* (left) and *Learning* (right)

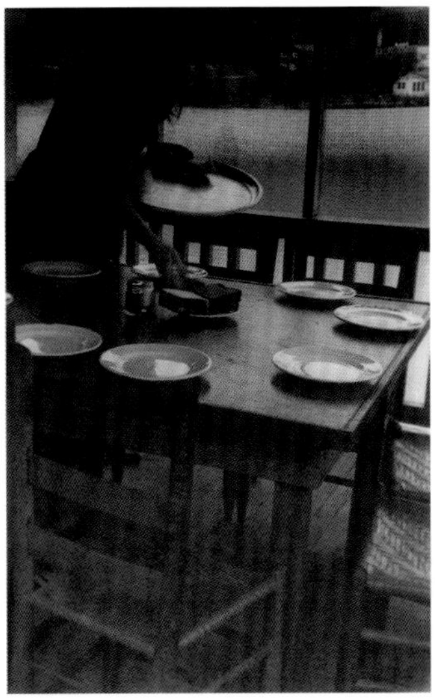

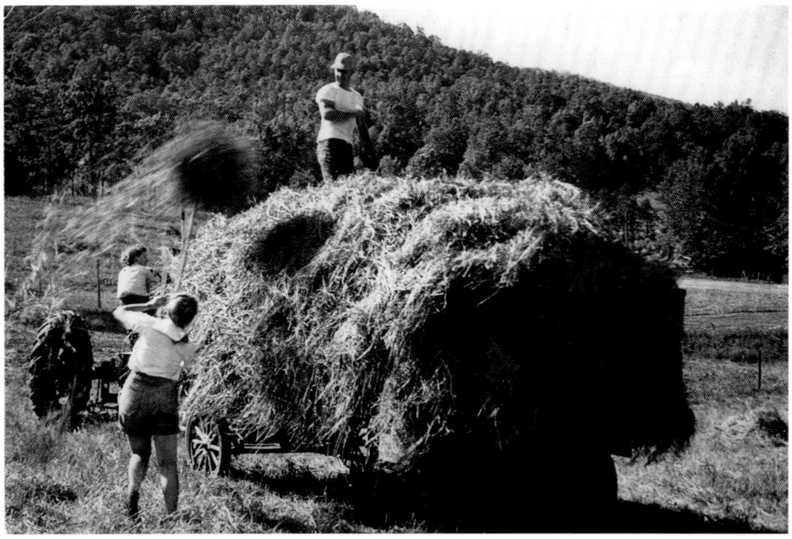

Setting a table in the Dining Hall

Students and farmer taking in hay

In a statement written at the time, which appeared in a publication made and printed by her in a limited edition at the college, Larsen described the principles according to which she taught:

> In the fall of 1949 photography was added to the art curriculum of Black Mountain College. Previously, during three summer institutes, Nancy and Beaumont Newhall had stimulated interest in photography, but never had it been offered as a part of a full year's correlated art program.
>
> Too often, I believe, the educational process has become a training of the memory in a rather parrot-like fashion. Very little emphasis has been placed on visual and acoustical training. As the result of required courses and curriculums starting immediately in the freshman year, most colleges turn out educated individuals in four years. I believe, more and more, that the educational process is almost a hands-off affair; not without guidance, of course, but providing the time and the opportunity for the opening and widening of channels for growth.
>
> Our photography courses have tried to proceed in this way. The courses in no way pretend to prepare the student for commercial or professional photography of any kind. The courses place emphasis not on taking the photograph, but the desire to take the photograph, with the photograph itself being the natural end result. It means that we are learning to see and become aware of life around us.
>
> This does not mean that we disregard thinking in design and the technical aspects of photography. On the contrary, the freedom to use technically beautiful instruments stems from competence, and respect for them. In the design of a photograph, which includes not only the photograph itself, but the thinking which precedes the shutter-clicking and carries over into the making of the final print, we try to go beyond the first step, away from the habitual, away from the unusual shot for the sake of being unusual, away from compositional tricks and shock devices. We do not use light meters; we believe that one can train oneself to see light under a variety of conditions.

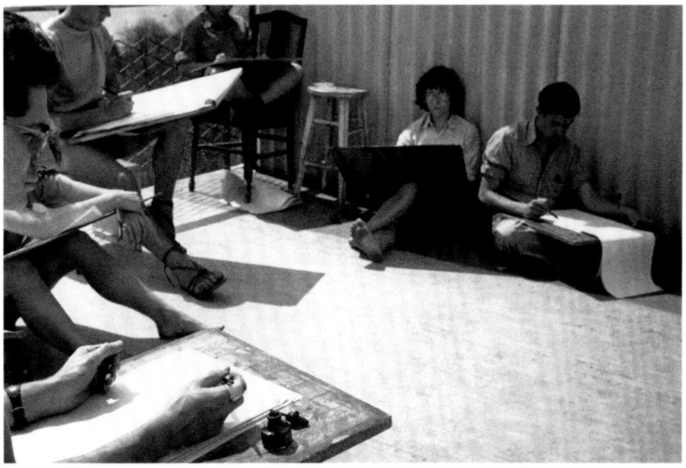

Drawing class on the roof of the Studies Building — Kenneth Noland far right

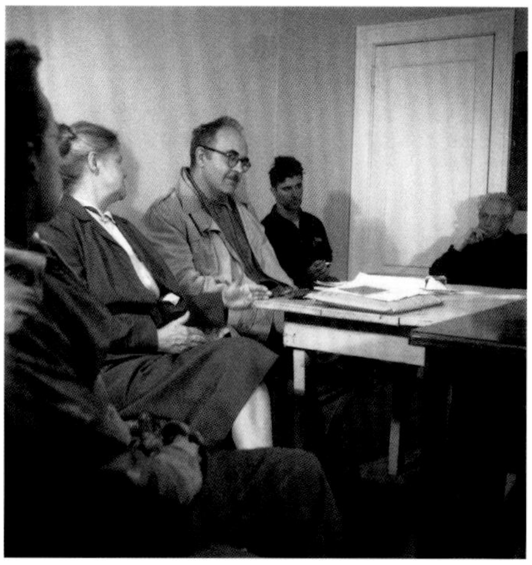

(from left) Leonard Billing, Nell Rice, Charles Olson, Joseph Fiore, Max Dehn

> With such considerations, each photograph cannot help but be a new experience. We make mistakes, many of them, but they serve to make us remember that we are constantly striving towards something, and we become even more in awe of this wonderful, mysterious process of making a picture.[7]

Larsen and some of the students in her class decided to produce a magazine, ***5 Photographers*** — actually a series of small monographs or portfolios, each devoted to the work of a single photographer. The five were Archer herself, Nick (Nicholas) Cernovitch, Andrew Oates, Vernon Phillips, and Stan VanDerBeek. (Cernovitch was to become one of the most celebrated lighting designers for dance and ballet companies; VanDerBeek became a leading experimental filmmaker.) Archer wrote in a preface:

> We at Black Mountain College interested in photography have decided to start a magazine. It started originally as a photography class project when we decided to try to put in order our thoughts and our work. Then came our desire to put it into magazine form.
>
> These are our aims as we see them now; we hope a year from now they will not be the same. We hope we will always be open for change.
>
> 1. to provide a means of communication between photographers
> 2. to promote interest in the spreading of creative photography
> 3. to promote educationally the inclusion of photography in the art department as well as the science department.
>
> We plan forthcoming issues on portraiture, history of photography, documentary photography, the work of individual photographers, landscapes, fashion photography, photography as education, etc.
>
> We hope this magazine will grow not by our asking you to contribute an article or a photograph but by your desire to do so. We hope that you will see enough in the magazine that you will want to do so.

This issue has been devoted to the photography being done at Black Mountain College; it is our starting point and the photography to which we are the closest. It is the work of four students and the photography instructor. The articles are not great essays but the result of trying to put our thoughts in order. Among ourselves we still disagree on some of the viewpoints and broad statements represented; if you do not agree with us we welcome your attempt to convince us otherwise.

Because of our financial condition, this issue has been limited to 25 copies, the text has been linotyped, and printed in our college print shop, and the cover lettered by hand, all the work of the photographers concerned. The magazine will live from issue to issue, with no long range program in mind. The photographs are original prints, for we wished to retain the original quality of the print. We also believe that making 25 prints of the same quality is a good discipline. We wish to explore the processes of reproduction in the hope of finding a fine reproductive method. Until then we will continue to use original prints.

Our aims and desires are as simple as that. Perhaps we are walking in shoes too big for our feet, but we believe it is a step in the right direction.[8]

(Copies of the publication are extremely rare; Andrew Oates says that he never got a copy for himself of his own monograph. The "forthcoming issues" never appeared.)

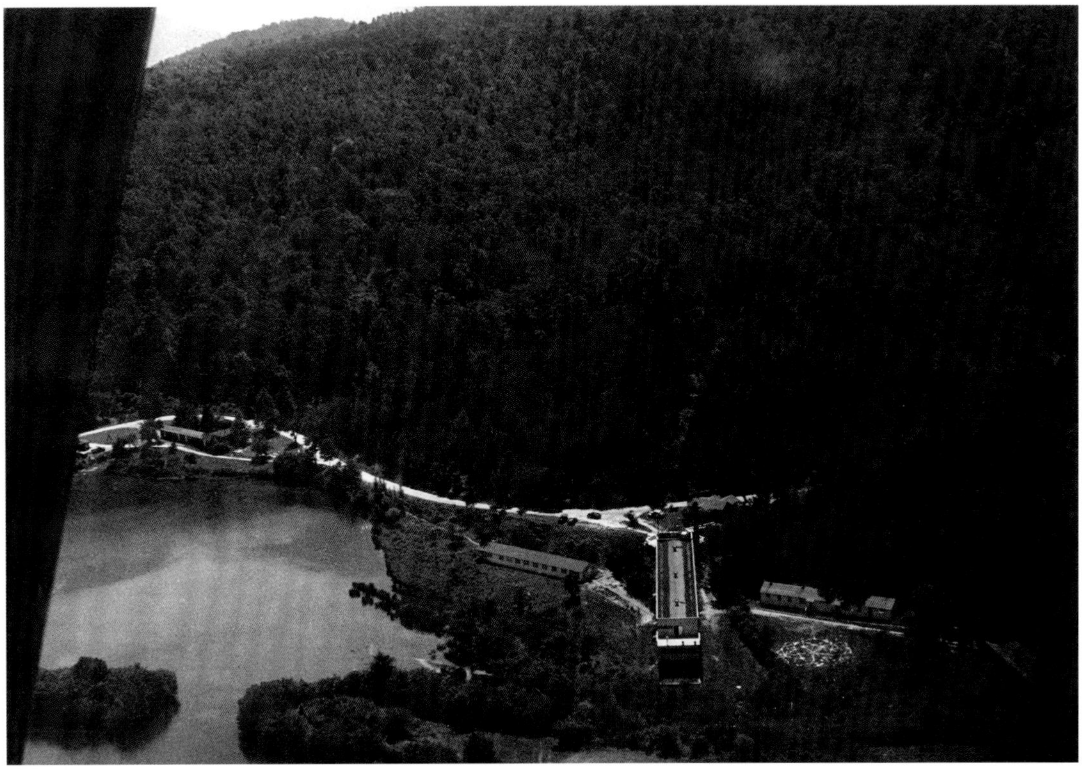

Aerial view of Lake Eden, the Studies Building, and Fuller's collapsed "Supine Dome" made from venetian blind strips, Summer 1948

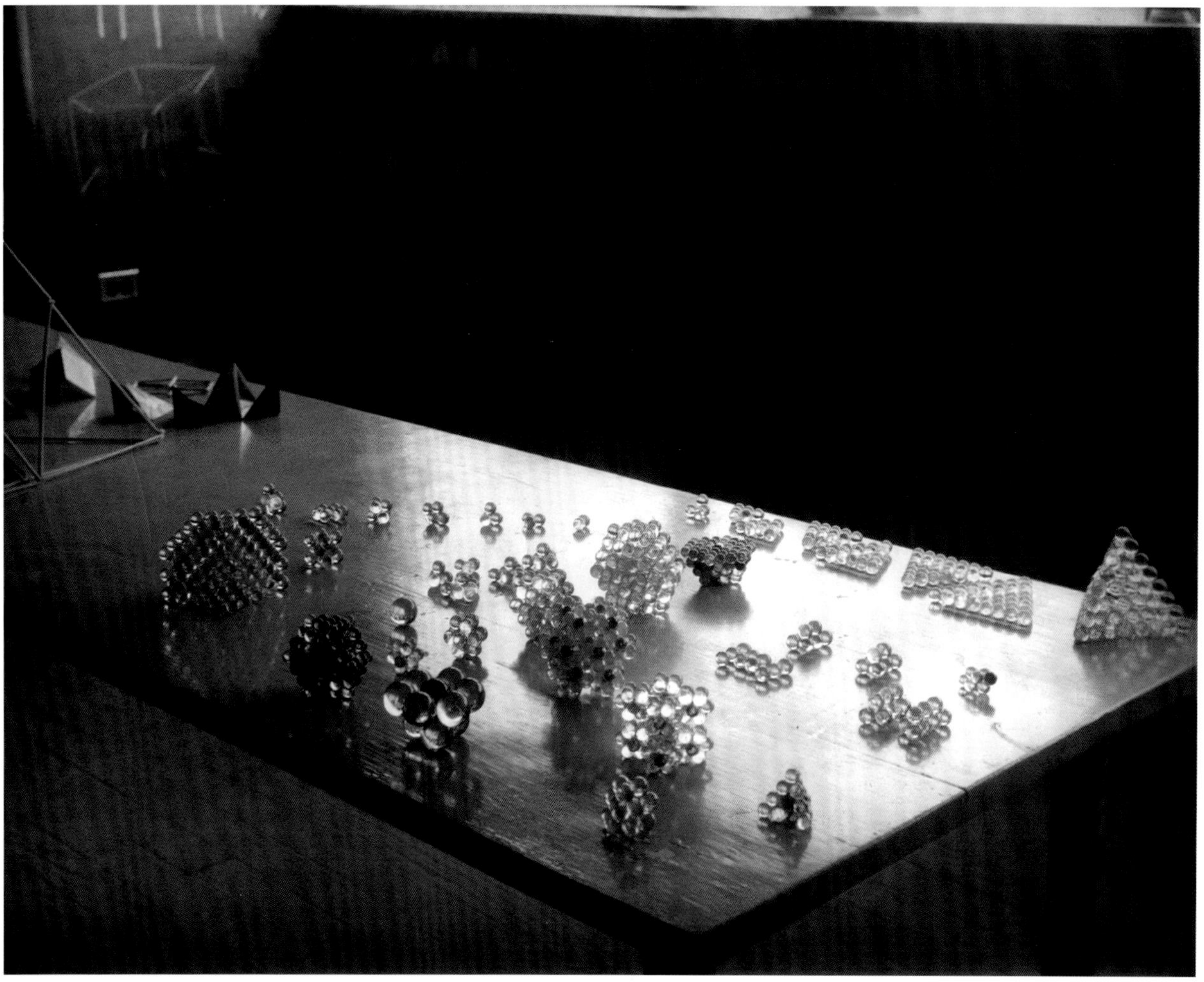

Buckminster Fuller's classroom

As is clear from Larsen's statement, her classes were very much in the Black Mountain spirit: Nick Cernovitch remembers her as being "very open — she gave us the material and sent us on our way." Although he was one of the "five photographers," he actually more or less gave up still photography when he found that he was sensitive to the chemicals used, which burned his hands, and "when the movie camera came along, I borrowed it, gave up all my classes, and devoted myself to filming." [9]

Andrew Oates was also not primarily a photographer — he studied weaving with Anni Albers (who had her students make their own looms) and continued to be a weaver for the rest of his working life. But he studied photography with Larsen, and when he was planning a trip to New York, she suggested that he take some of his work to the Museum of Modern Art. He accordingly made an appointment to see Edward Steichen, then director of the museum's photography department. Coincidentally, Steichen had been approached by the Polio Foundation, who asked him to select five photographers who suffered from the disease in order to provide images for posters that would be distributed throughout the United States to raise money for the foundation. As a result, Larsen was chosen and received $500 for her work. (Her students tried to help her overcome the effects of polio: Cernovitch gave her exercises, the Jennerjahns massaged her feet.) Steichen also offered to be the examiner for Oates' own graduation project, and came to the college when he was paying a visit to Carl Sandburg, his brother-in-law, who lived in nearby Flat Rock.[10] Larsen's work was later exhibited at the Museum of Modern Art, as was that of Oates and Robert Rauschenberg, another of her students.

Larsen left Black Mountain in 1953; in September of that year she married Charles Archer, a student at the college. They moved to the village of Black Mountain, where Larsen maintained a studio until 1956, taking mostly family portraits. From July 1954 to June 1955 she was in Washington DC for a year of what she described as "self-directed study at the Library of Congress... [in the] photographic archives of the Farm Security Administration and the Maya of Central America,"[11] following which the couple moved to Tucson, Arizona.

She devoted the rest of her life to education. Although her work had been shown at the Photo League and the Museum of Modern Art in New York, she stopped exhibiting after 1957. To make money, she took portrait photographs, then in the 1960s once again started to work outside, "photographing light" at a particular time of day.[12] In Arizona she was first Director of Adult Education at the Tucson Art Center, then director and teacher at the Hidden Springs School; she was also on the faculty of Pima Community College, and was instrumental in the foundation of a small liberal arts college, Avalon College. Larsen moved to Santa Fe in 1975 "to be quiet, and write, and work further on developing perceptually based educational programs."[13]

In 1979, with her daughter, Erika Zarow, she initiated the Institutes for the Release of Potential. Zarow says that her mother's teaching methods were deeply influenced by the experience of studying at Black Mountain with Albers and Fuller, and were always concerned with the processes of perception.[14] Larsen wrote several studies of these processes, which remain unpublished. She was licensed by Fuller to develop Dymaxion Principles; something that she insisted upon in her educational work was that every child in every class (kindergarten through Sixth Grade) be taught Geometry. The program, she wrote, was "first greeted with some suspicion and hostility because there is a prevailing concept that most children do not easily respond to Geometry (especially the very young), [but] because of its results, [it] ended up being enthusiastically received, with some puzzlement as to why."[15] (One of her manuscript studies was called ***Geometry: The Synergistic Relationship of the Five Regular Polyhedra***.)

She died in 2001. Zarow grew up hearing about Black Mountain: Josef Albers, Buckminster Fuller, Merce Cunningham, John Cage, and Robert Rauschenberg were "household names." She remembers attending a Black Mountain reunion with her mother and being impressed by the fact that many of the people there spoke of Archer herself as a key figure at the school, a teacher who opened their eyes so that nothing was ever the same again.

This essay was originally published in a slightly different form in ***Aperture***, issue no. 179, Summer 2005.

David Vaughan is the archivist of the Cunningham Dance Foundation and the author of ***Merce Cunningham: Fifty Years*** (Aperture, 1997) and ***Frederick Ashton and his Ballets*** (revised edition, Dance Books, 1999). He received the 2000 CORD (Congress on Research in Dance) Award for Outstanding Leadership in Dance Research, and in 2001 a New York Dance and Performance Award ("Bessie") for sustained achievement.

[1] Mary Emma Harris, The Arts at Black Mountain College (Cambridge MA and London, England: The MIT Press, 1987), p.245.

[2] Information from an unpublished autobiographical portrait by Larsen; I am indebted to Mary Emma Harris for further biographical and other information.

[3] Harris, p.146.

[4] Conversation with Andrew Oates, 1 June 2004.

[5] Conversation with Elizabeth and W.P. Jennerjahn, 24 May 2004.

[6] Autobiographical portrait.

[7] Hazel-Freida [sic] Larsen, Photography at Black Mountain College, n.d.

[8] Hazel-Frieda Larsen, 5 Photographers, n.d.

[9] Conversation with Nicholas Cernovitch, 28 May 2004.

[10] Conversation with Andrew Oates, 1 June 2004.

[11] Autobiographical portrait.

[12] Ibid.

[13] Ibid.

[14] Conversation with Erika Zarow, 27 May 2004.

[15] Autobiographical portrait.

# CAPTURING LIGHT

BY ERIKA ZAROW

Every day, for a number of years, people would come to our house to have my mother take their picture. At that time, in the mid-sixties, it was unusual for a photographer to use natural light for a portrait sitting, or to work outdoors. It all started with one woman who saw the portraits Hazel did at Black Mountain College and wanted to be photographed by her. My mother did not feel advertising was necessary, that the right people would always come together. By word of mouth they found their way to our door. There were important people, schoolgirls, mothers with children, brides, and children alone.

Our backyard was like a jungle, with overgrown trees, their branches sweeping the ground. In the afternoon the leaves would be drenched in light, the perfect time for taking pictures. It was my job to keep the sunspots off the face, taking care to leave some light to play in the hair or hold a branch from view. She would say, "now tilt your head somewhat, but bring your eyes back this way." Patiently, she watched, as the person visibly relaxed, and seemed to slowly reveal themselves to her. As I watched the dappled light moving with the trees, my mind would record with my eyes the picture she saw with her camera.

At night there was the sound of the reels of film being developed, rhythmically tipping back and forth in the metal canisters. Then I would study the images from that day on the film as it hung from clothes hangers. She would let me snap the heavy metal clips at the bottom to hang them straight to dry. If it was not too late I would sit in the yellow light of the darkroom while she timed the first exposure, the negative image crisp on the white paper. With the paper first placed face down in the developing tray, we would turn it over and wait for the magic to appear. Slowly the face would emerge, then the trees, and I would see the picture that earlier that day my mind had recorded, but now seen through her eyes. The ordinary people became extraordinary, luminous and poised.

Around that age, 9 or 10, I also began to sit in on my mother's classes, sometimes out of boredom, at the Tucson Art Center. The classes were held in a huge room with floor to ceiling windows on one side and a baby grand piano in the corner. I listened, consciously, to what she had to say, and was intrigued by the occasional wild and excited outbursts from the students.

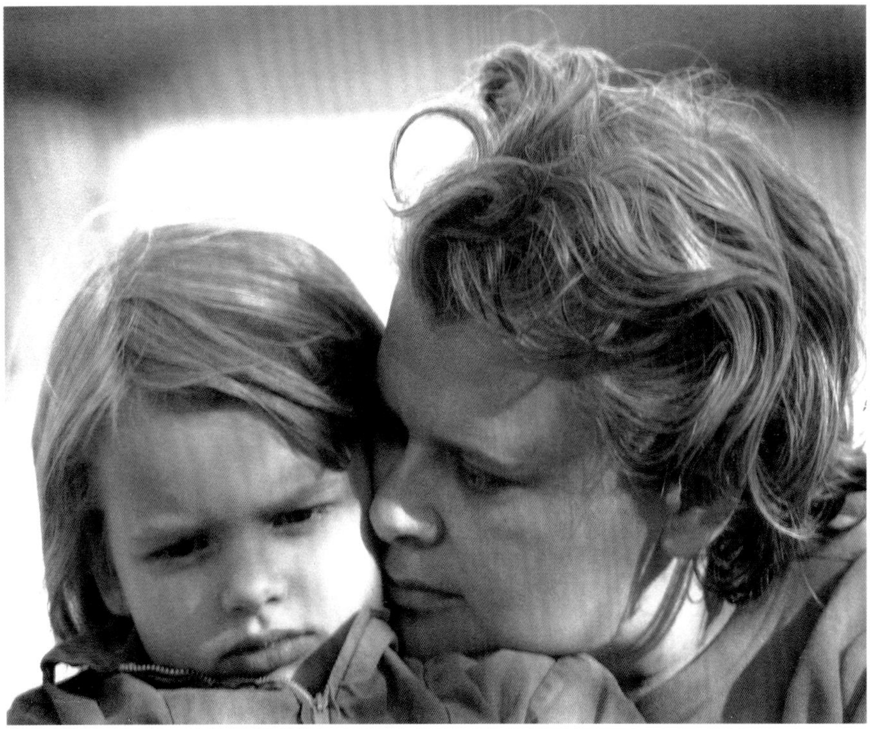

Archer with her daughter Erika

*Perception*, or *Learning to See*, subtitled *Things Are Not What They Appear To Be or There Is Another Way*, was at the basis of all that she taught. She maintained that if you set up a camera facing the broad side of a barn and 10 different people looked through the viewfinder, clicked the shutter and each developed their own picture, that you would have 10 uniquely different photographs. The camera faithfully records not only what is in front of it, but what is behind it as well. With exercises in observation, the students learned the difference between seeing and identification. Attending the photography class was a retired Army doctor. Agitated, he would stand up and say, "Mrs. Archer, are you telling me I can't see? This is a piano right here." He then described the piano, slapping it with his hand. Very patiently she would reply, "Yes, Doctor, you have competently identified the thing, but you have not seen it!"

Slowly the frustration would subside as she asked each student to describe what he or she saw. She spoke of linguistics, how the words we use bring forth images, which are of the known. To see freshly, to see something new, we must understand how some words allow seeing to take place, while others are hindrances to perception. She often quoted Buckminster Fuller: "The rose probably has a very extraordinary function in the Universe, but the name is a hindrance."

As the students responded, Hazel pointed out the difference between an observation and a comment, which usually contains a value judgement based on polarities: good/bad, beautiful/ugly, likes and dislikes. Polarities deny our giving full attention to what we are observing because our mind is occupied with measuring and comparing to an acquired body of knowledge. Learning to see involved unlearning the habitual, our unconscious tendencies to act reflexively from past experience. Using tools of the known (identification, criticism and analysis) keeps us from entering into an intimate relationship with what we are observing. An observation, however, is impersonal, and assumes nothing, stating simply what is. It does not filter new information. Pure observation puts thinking on hold, creating a stillness, fully alert, that allows seeing to take place without interference from the mind.

"How will we know when we are seeing?" they would ask. "If you watch your process, you will know" she would say, "because there will be a surprise. The new comes as a surprise, a shock, illumination, and, very often, revelation."

Within the process of observing one's self observing, the running commentary subsides and a conscious observer emerges. In this state, we move beyond the realm of the five senses, and what we are observing becomes a direct experience of the thing itself. We become receptive, able to receive, and responsive, able to respond; it is through this exchange that we have a firsthand experience, and we are changed by it. A painting or photograph is a communication of the experience and becomes a natural, not manufactured or constructed, by-product of the experience itself.

She wrote of this process:

> The merging of the exquisite
> relationships of heart (responding)
> (drawing near to) Something;
> hand (touching-physical) and eye (seeing the surface)
> now touching with the eye,
> then penetrating that surface to the invisible

As the group continued to describe what they saw, you could feel an undercurrent of excitement. "We may see something as a cup or a mountain," she said, "but we must understand that, essentially, we are interpreting light. Information is contained in light, and when we are receptive, we become like the camera itself; we capture light."

Very often someone would get up and shout, "Yes! Yes! I get it! I see what you mean!" Sometimes that person never returned to class. Hazel believed that this is the essence of learning. It is a transformational process that does not take place over time. When we see, it is instantaneous, and the world is new.

My mother wrote these words about the learning experience:

> Real learning has to do with the awakening and the remembrance of individual destiny. The teacher is an usher and is standing by to nurture. Nurturing really means loving — an impersonal love which comes into being when one begins to hold in abeyance (which is extremely difficult in the beginning), the comment and any kind of measurement that would bring forth criticism. Love, indeed, is blind. It is the same love of full attention that Parsifal was finally able to offer the grievously wounded Fisher King that brought about the King's healing and dissolving of the wasteland. Fullness is restored; a metanoia has occurred. All loving is the process of metanoia at work. It is the most direct communication that exists.

Erika Zarow is Hazel Larsen Archer's daughter.

# HANDS

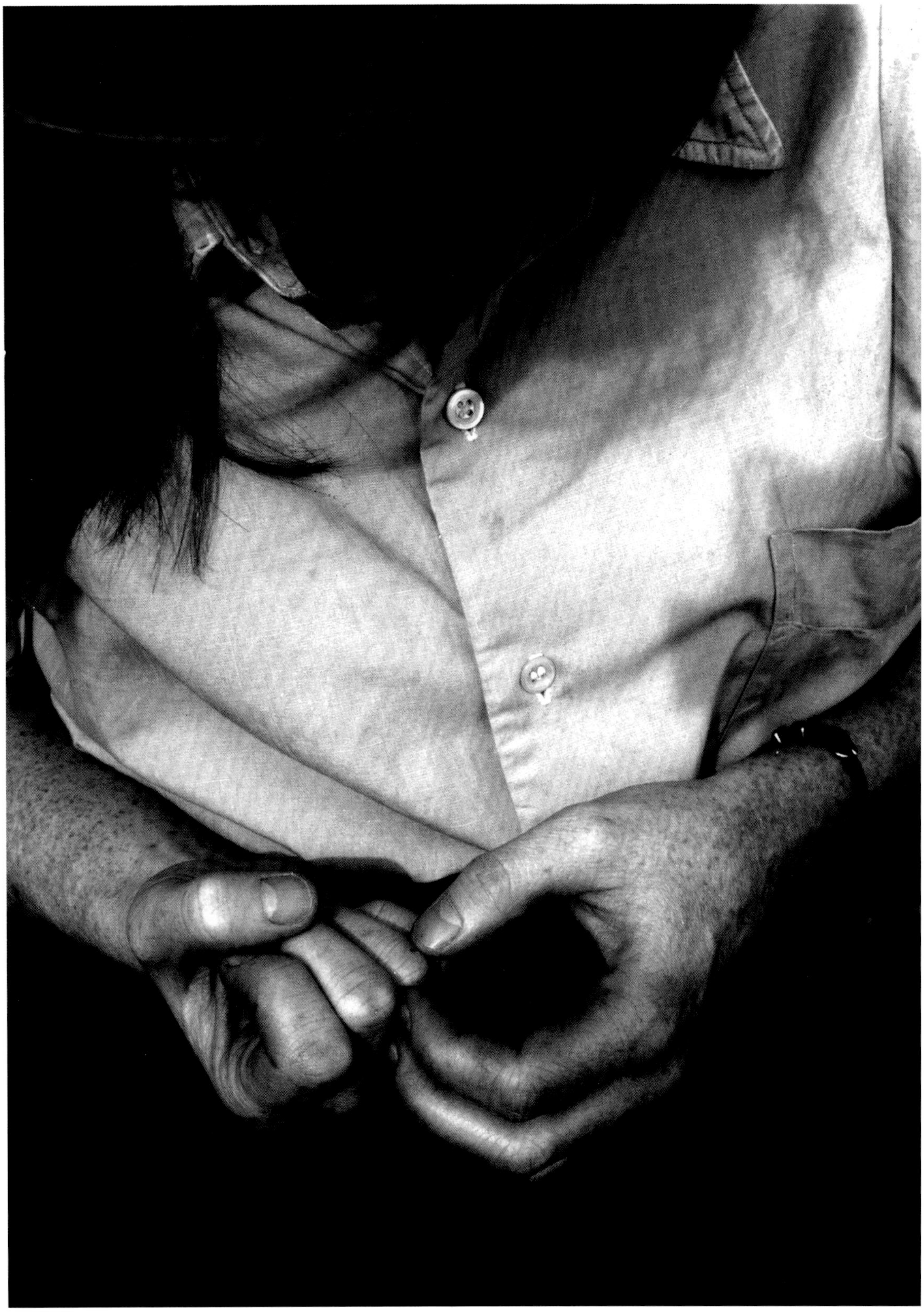

Untitled

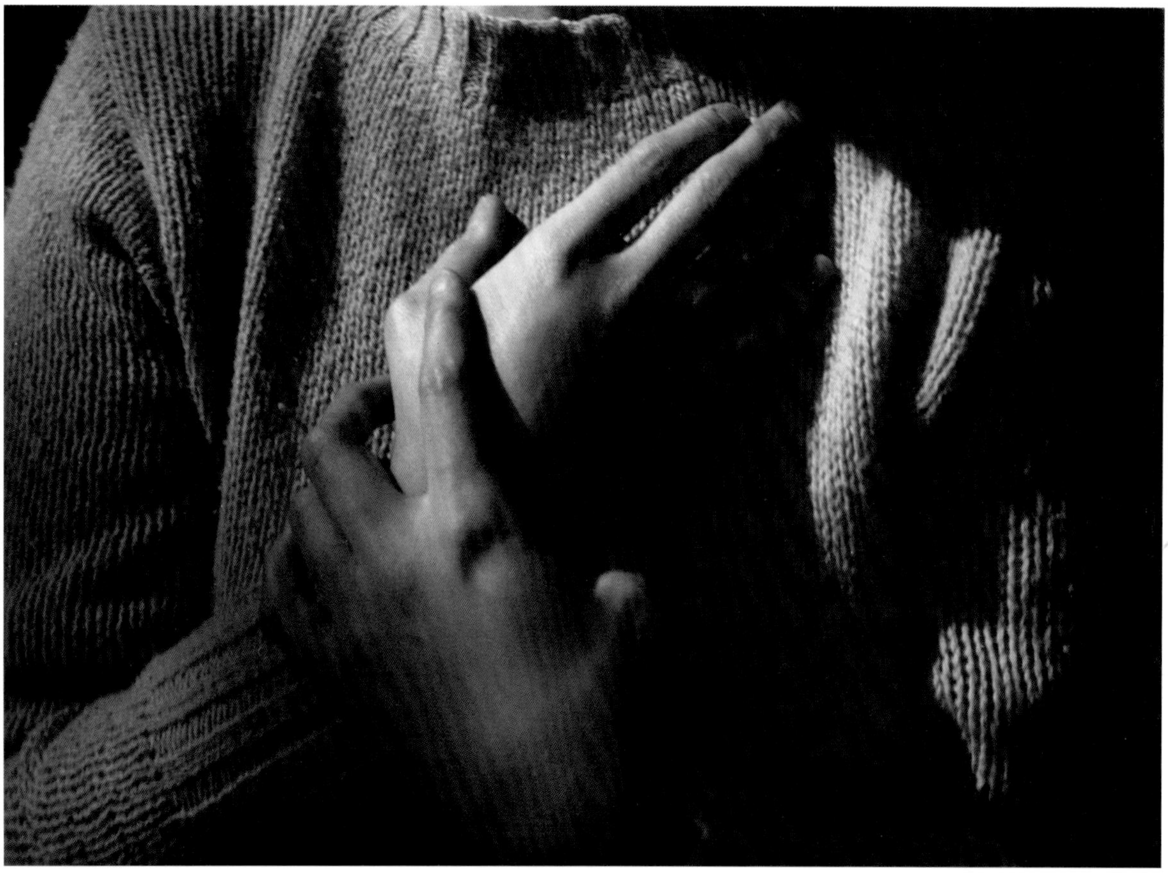

Untitled

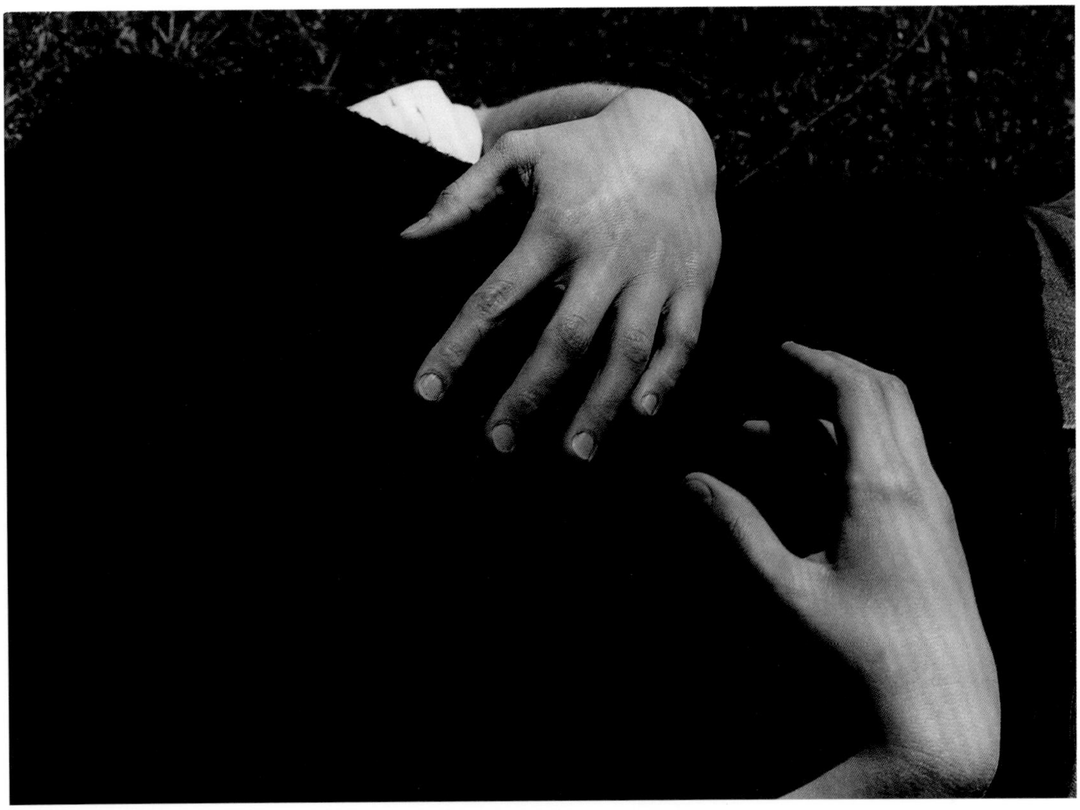

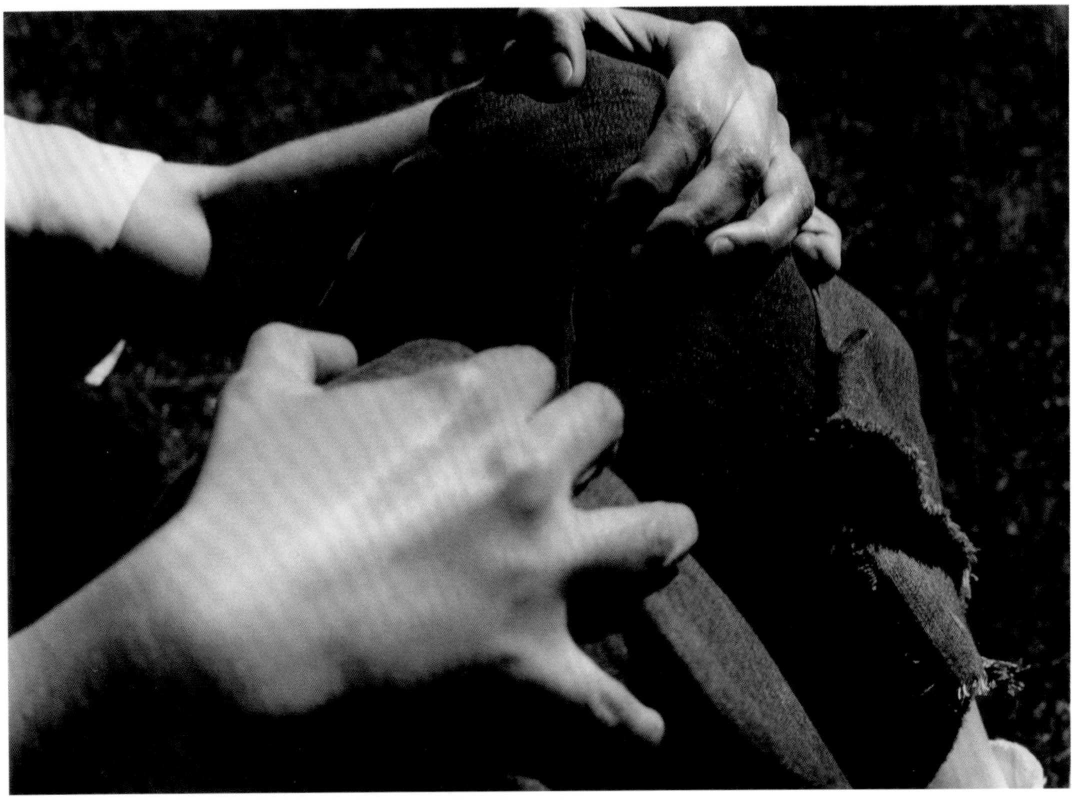

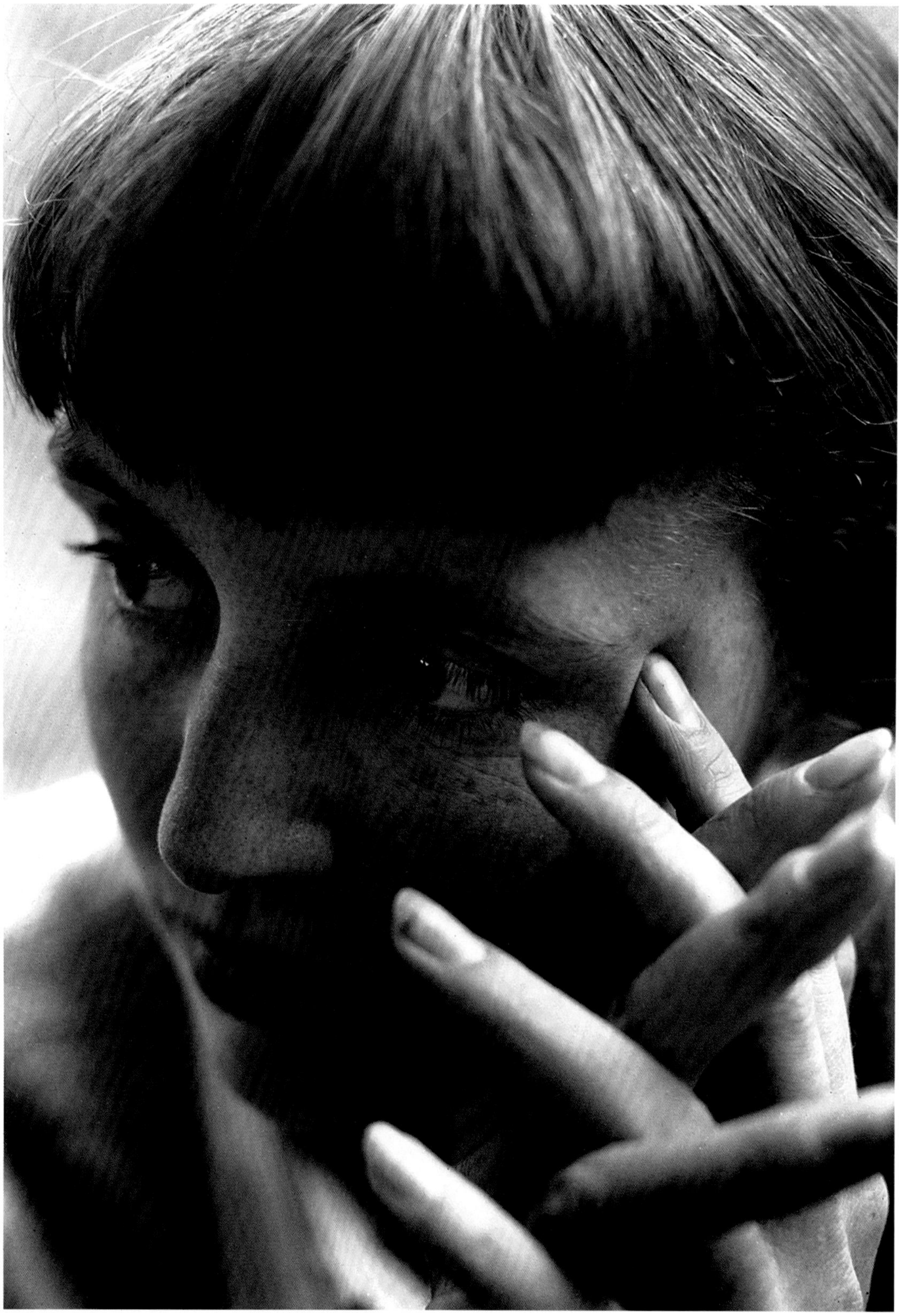

Joan Stack

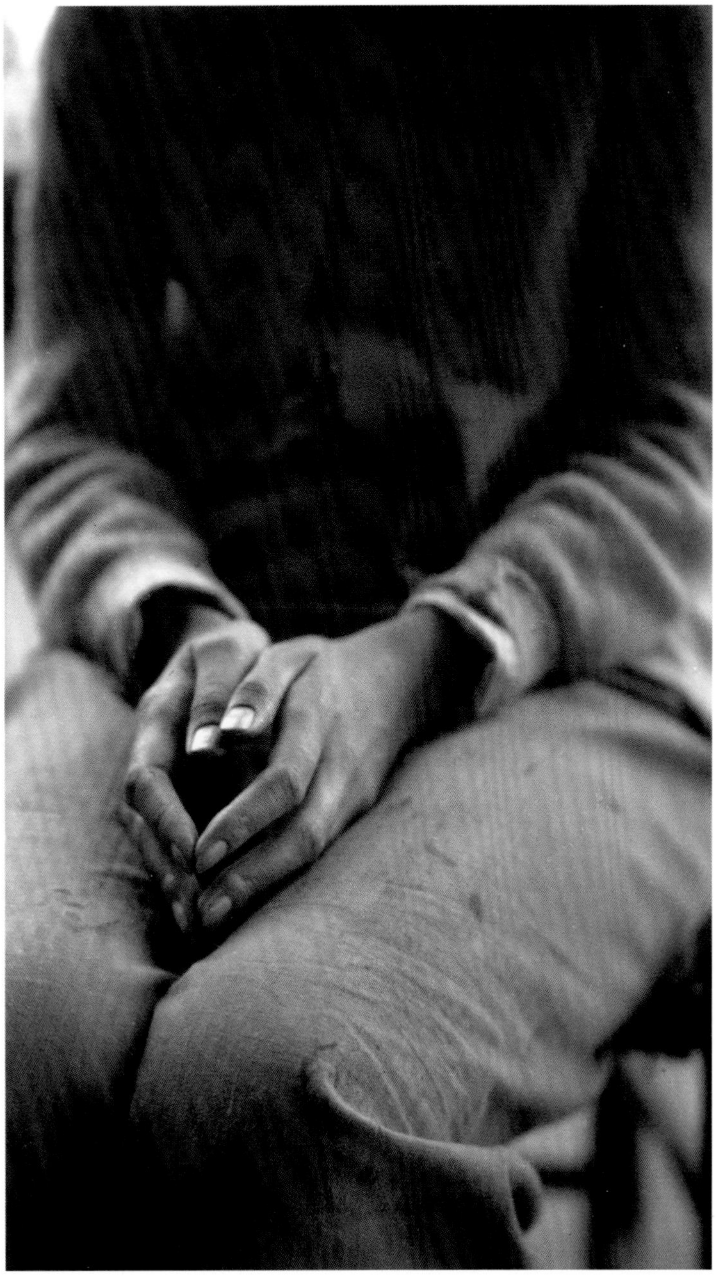

Untitled

# QUIET HOUSE

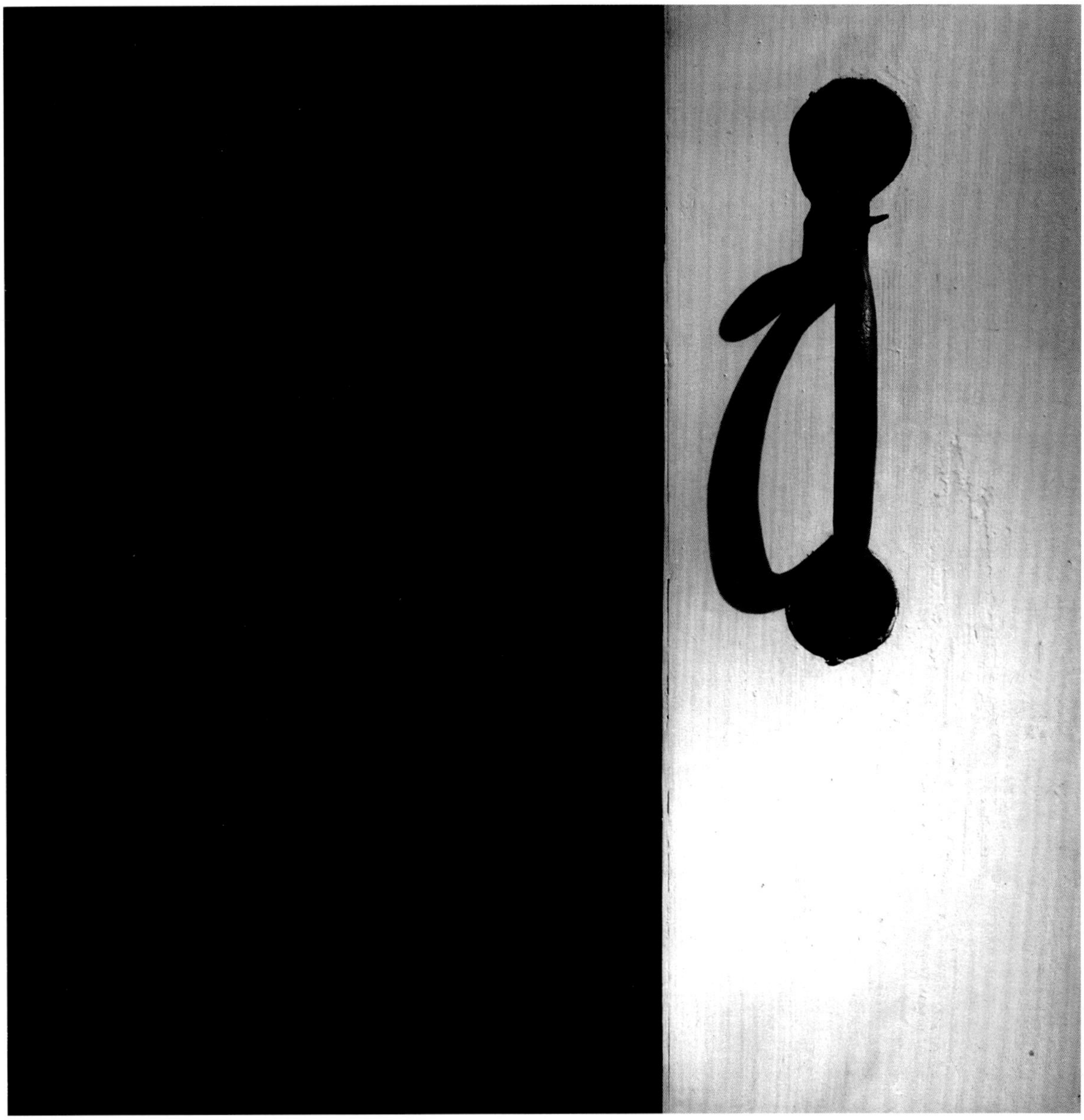

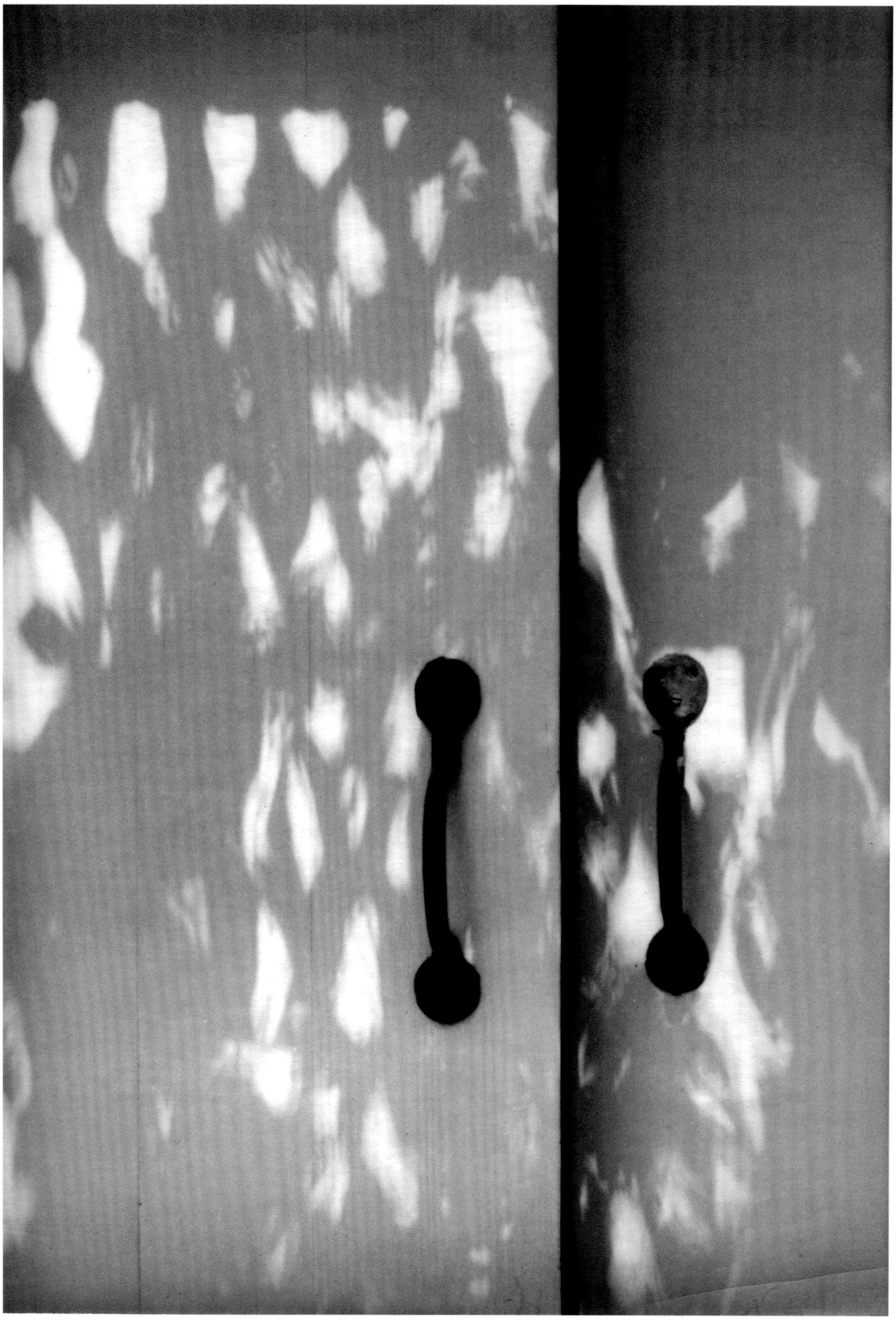

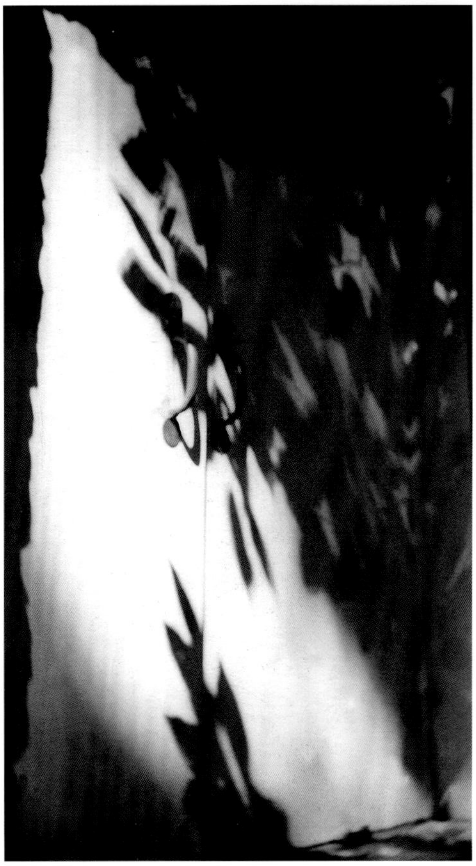

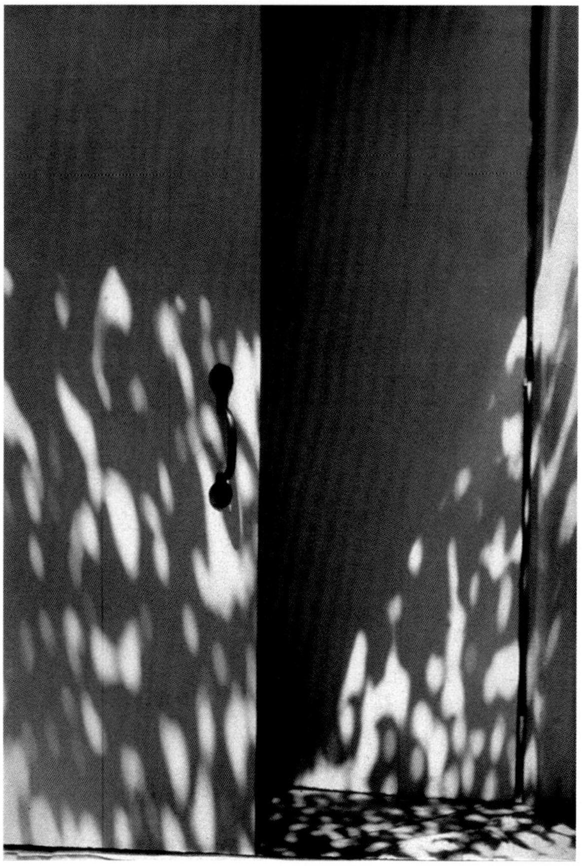

Black Mountain College Museum + Arts Center Collection

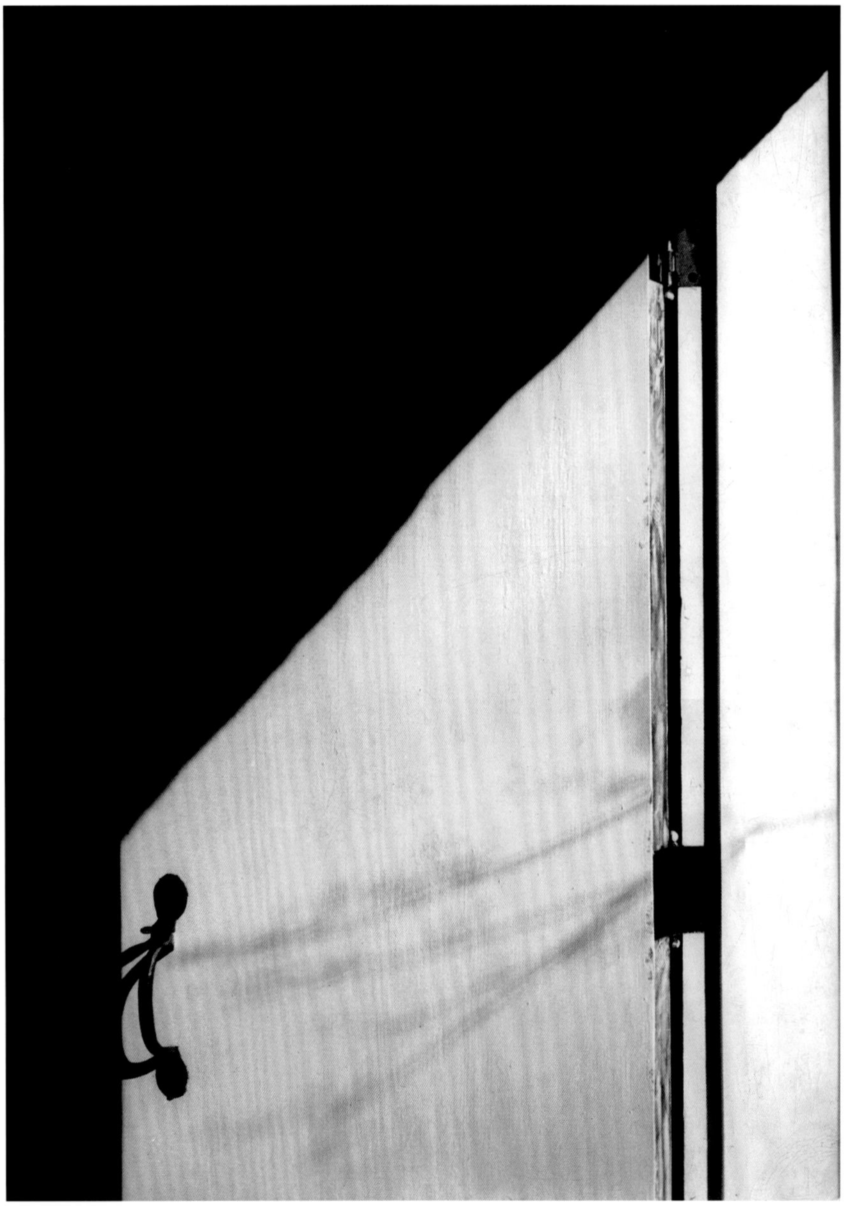

Quiet House Doors

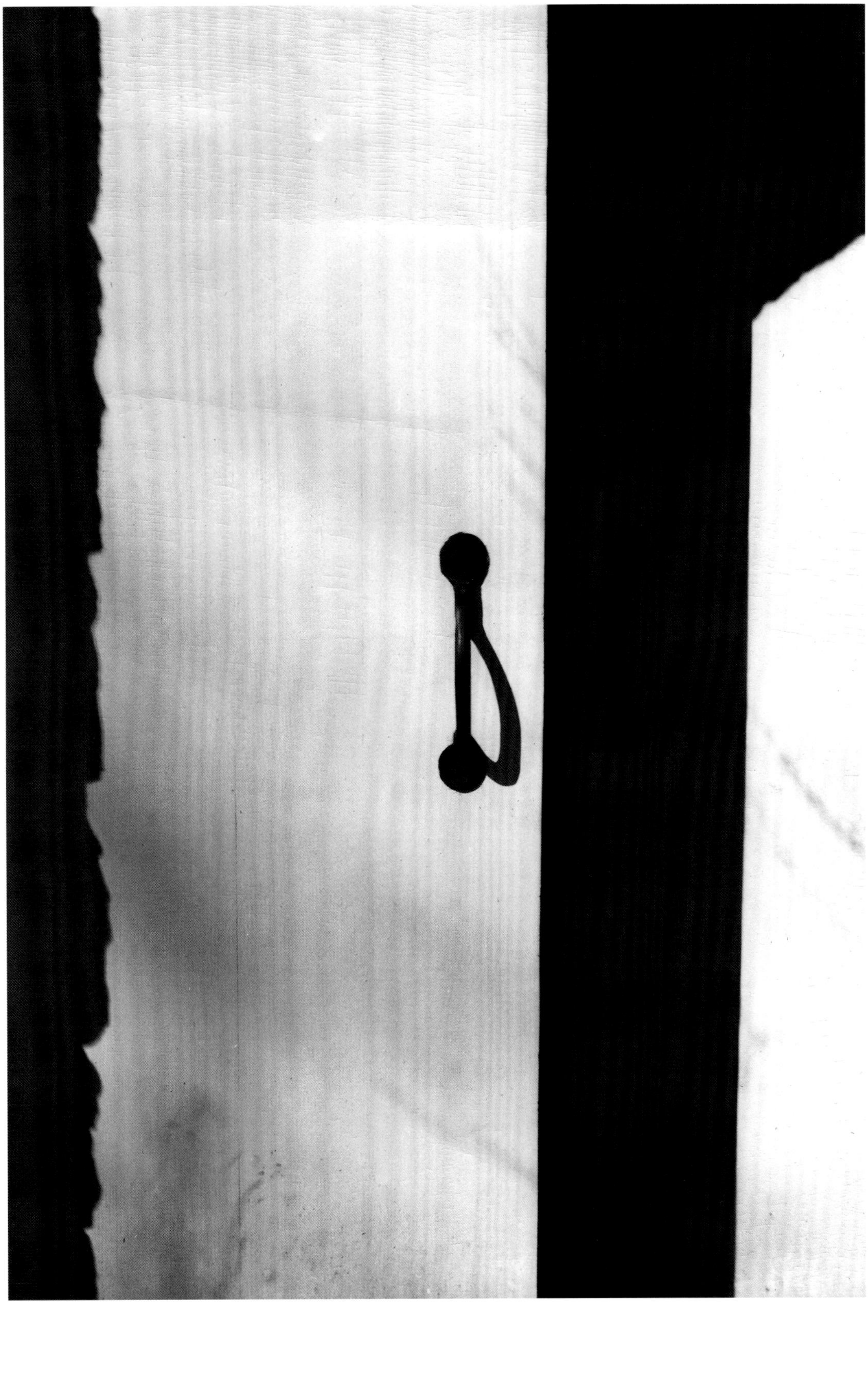

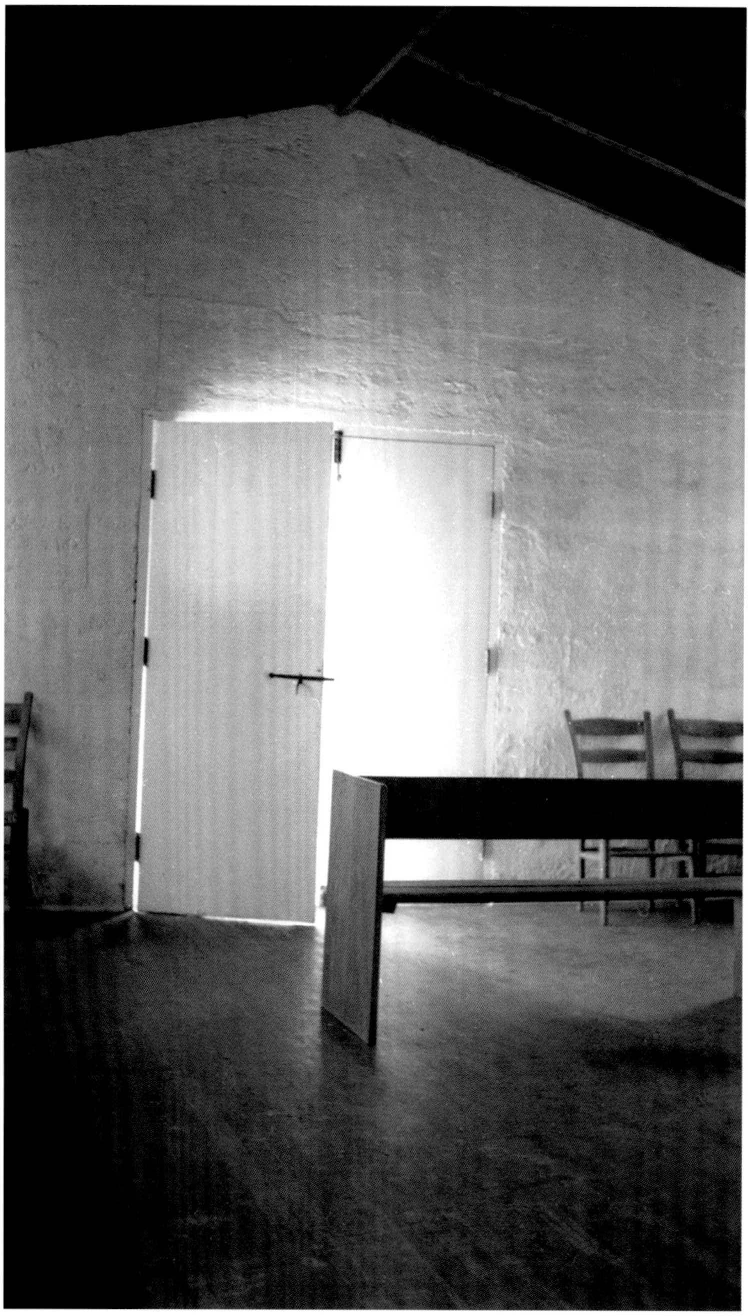

Quiet House Interior

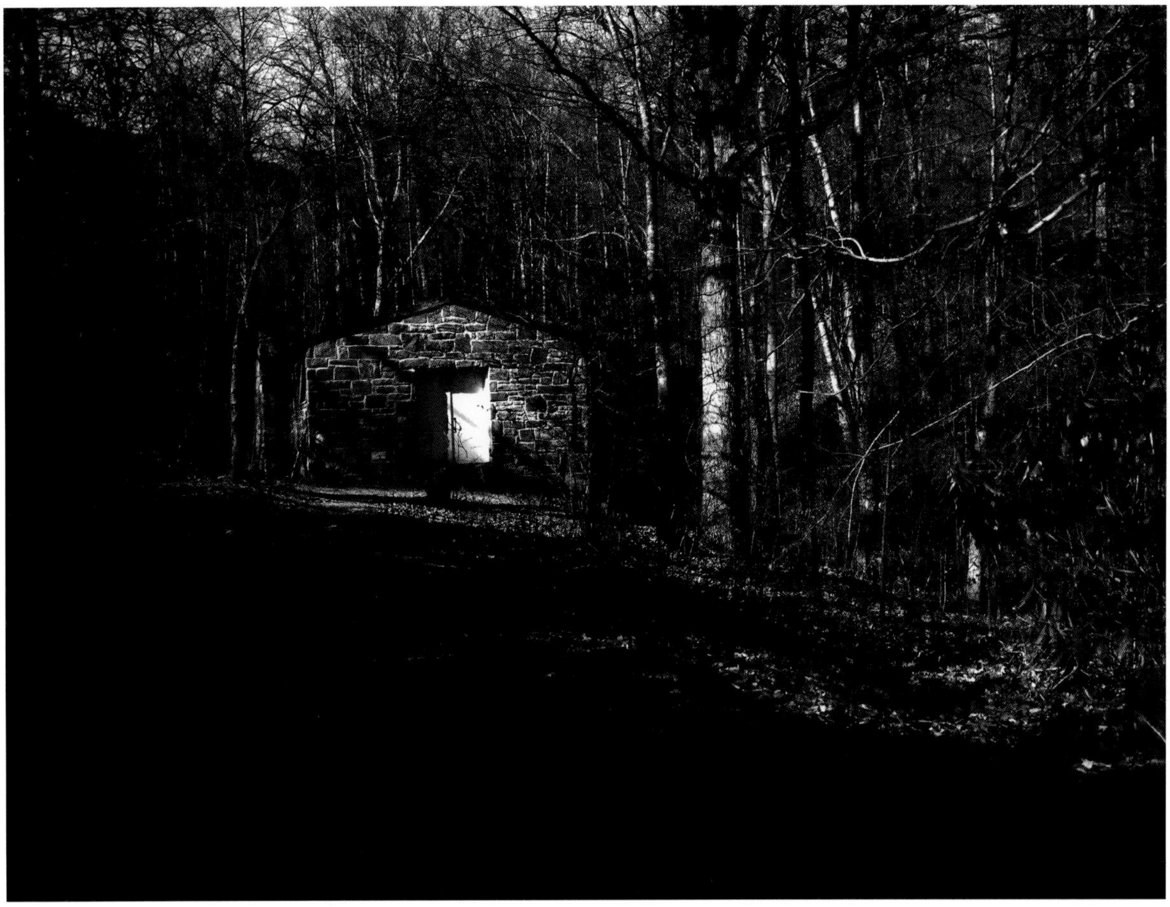

This simple structure, reminiscent of a Quaker Meetinghouse, was designed and built by former BMC student Alex Reed in memory of a faculty child, nine year old Mark Dreier, who died in an accident involving the college truck. The Quiet House was a place for contemplation, meditation, and the observance of special occasions.

Quiet House on the BMC campus

# DANCE / THEATRE / MUSIC

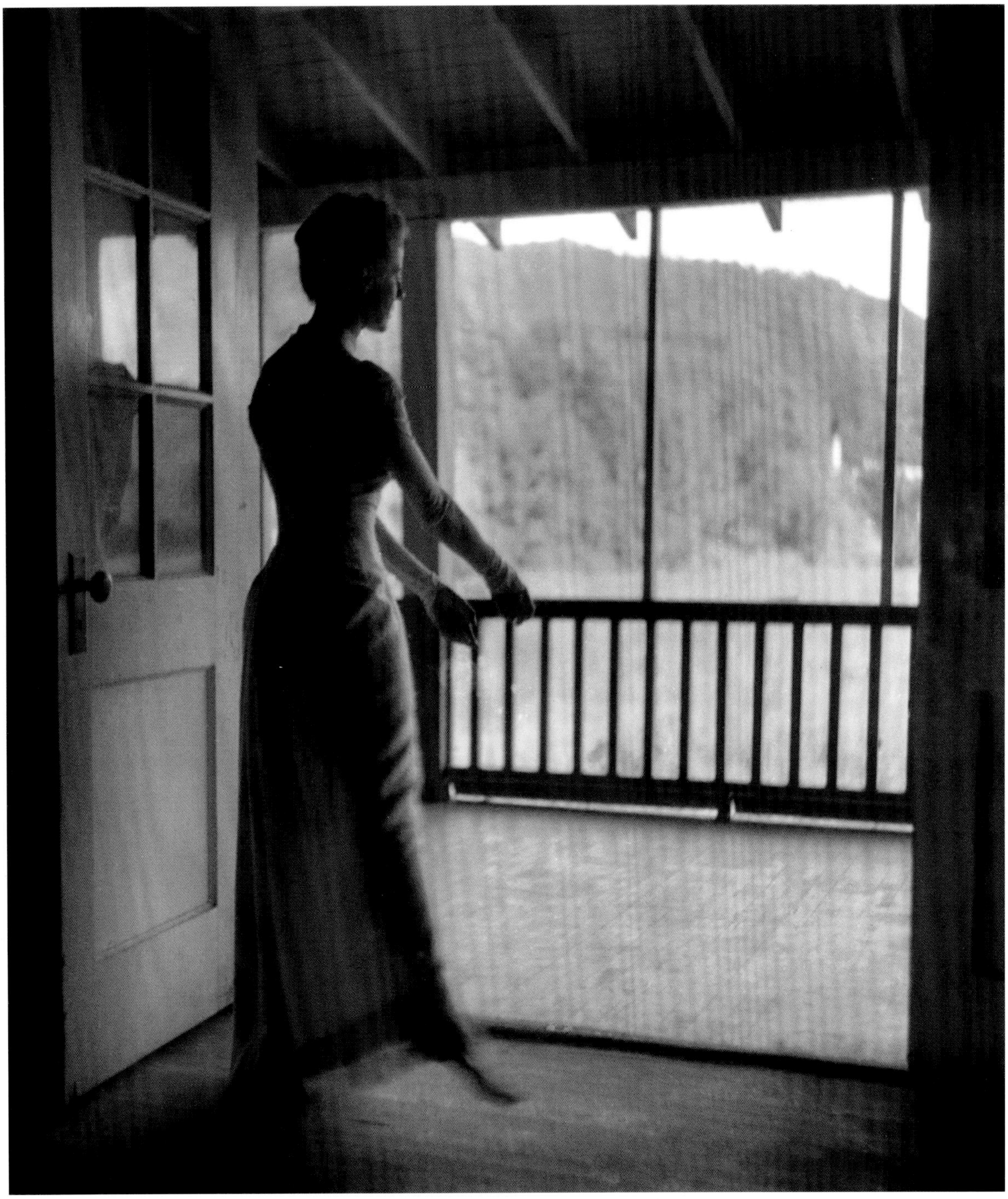

Katherine Litz in the Dining Hall

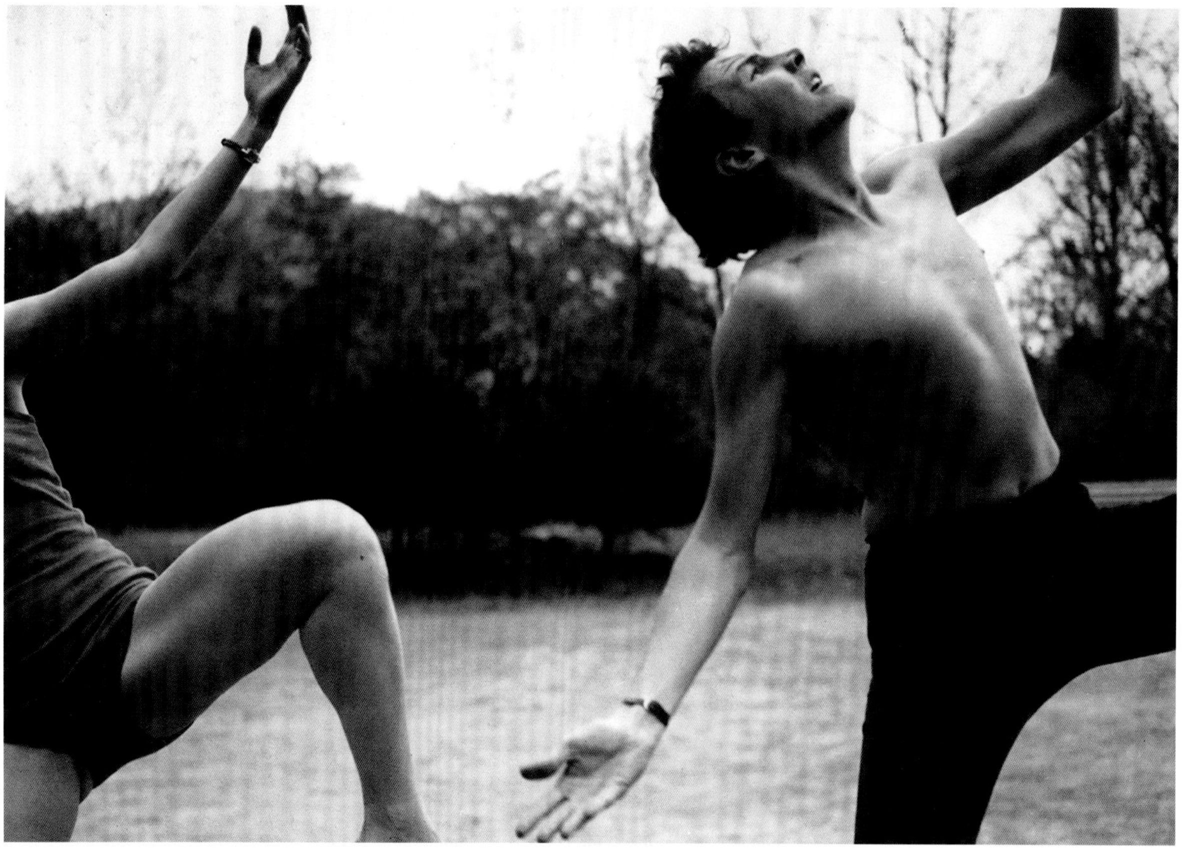

Elizabeth Schmitt Jennerjahn and Robert Rauschenberg

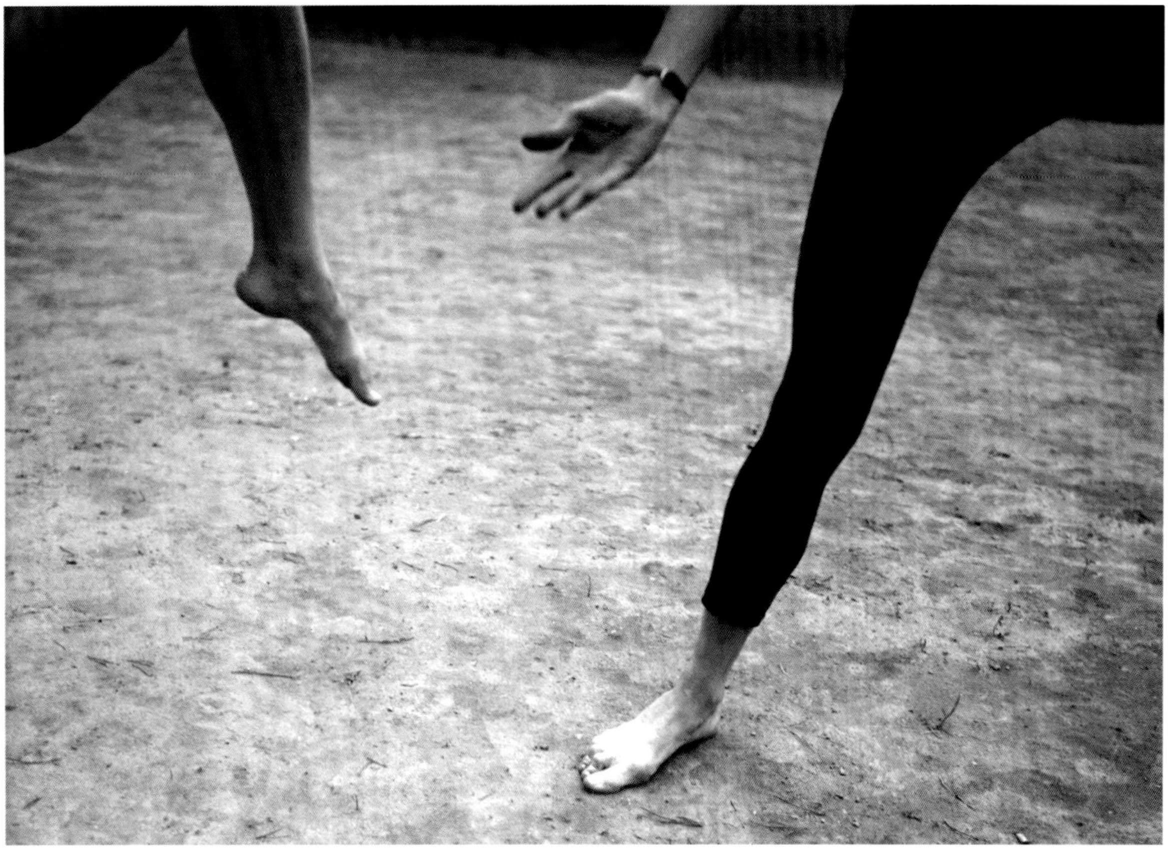

Elizabeth Schmitt Jennerjahn and Robert Rauschenberg

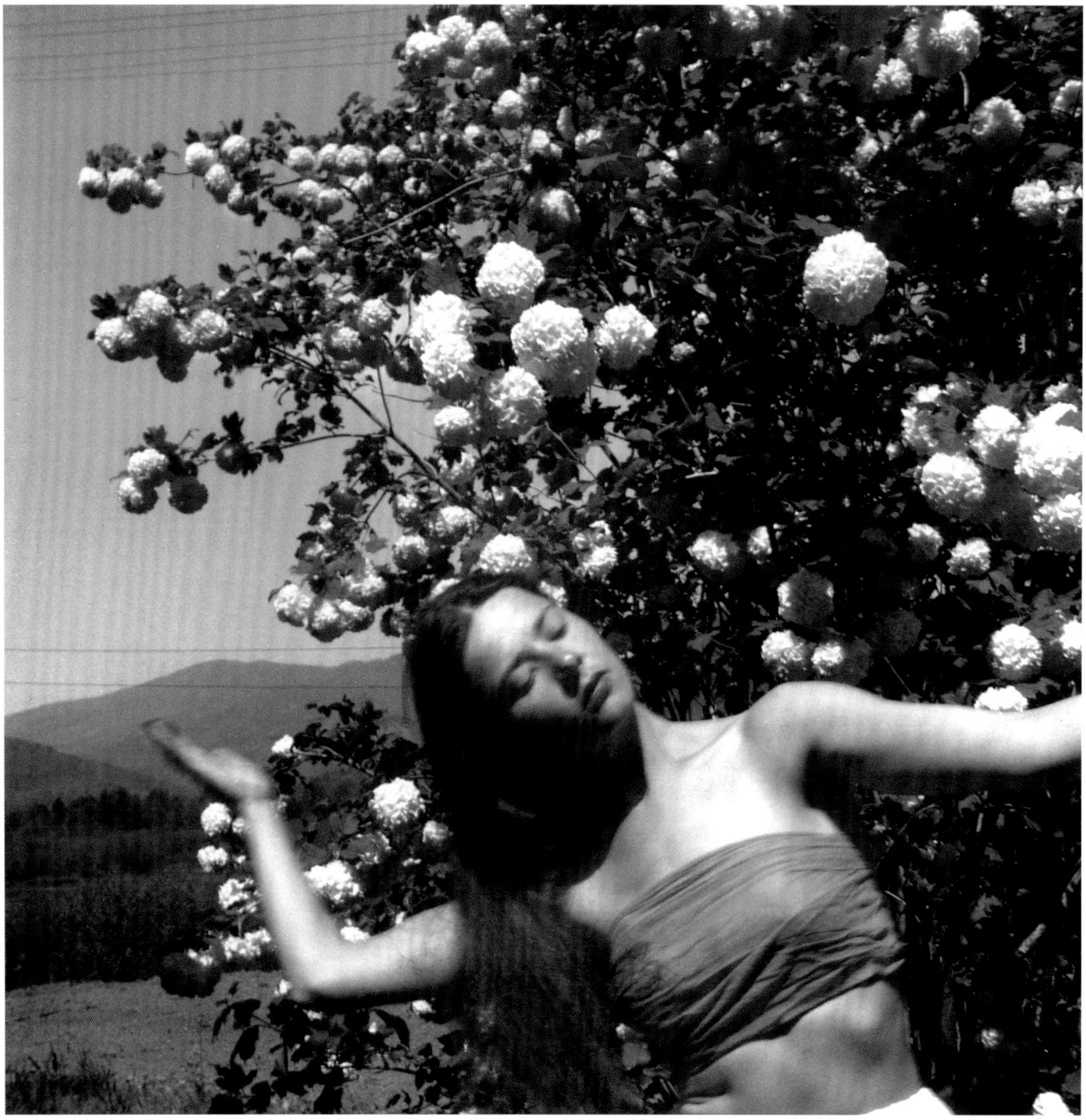

Elizabeth Schmitt Jennerjahn

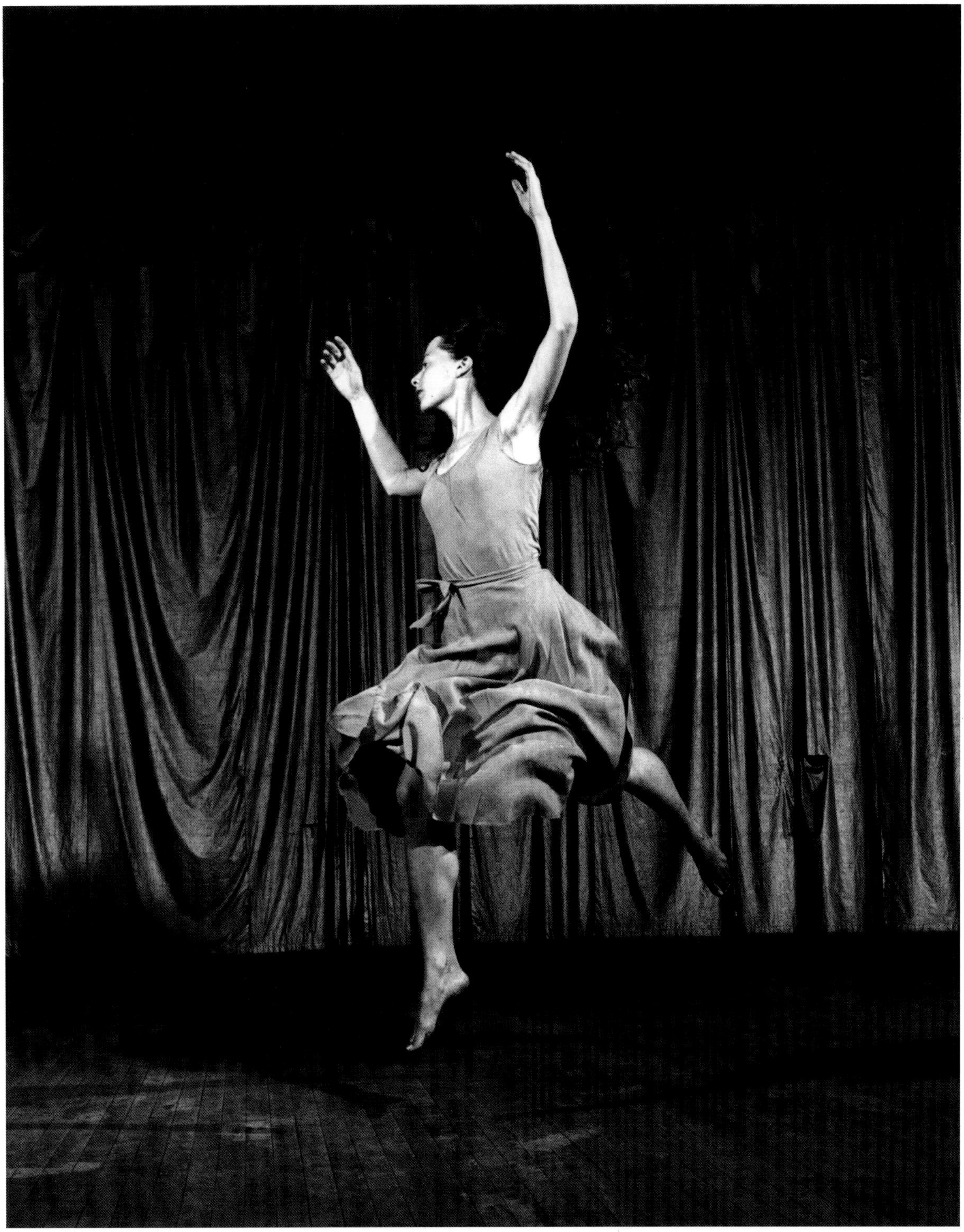

Elizabeth Schmitt Jennerjahn

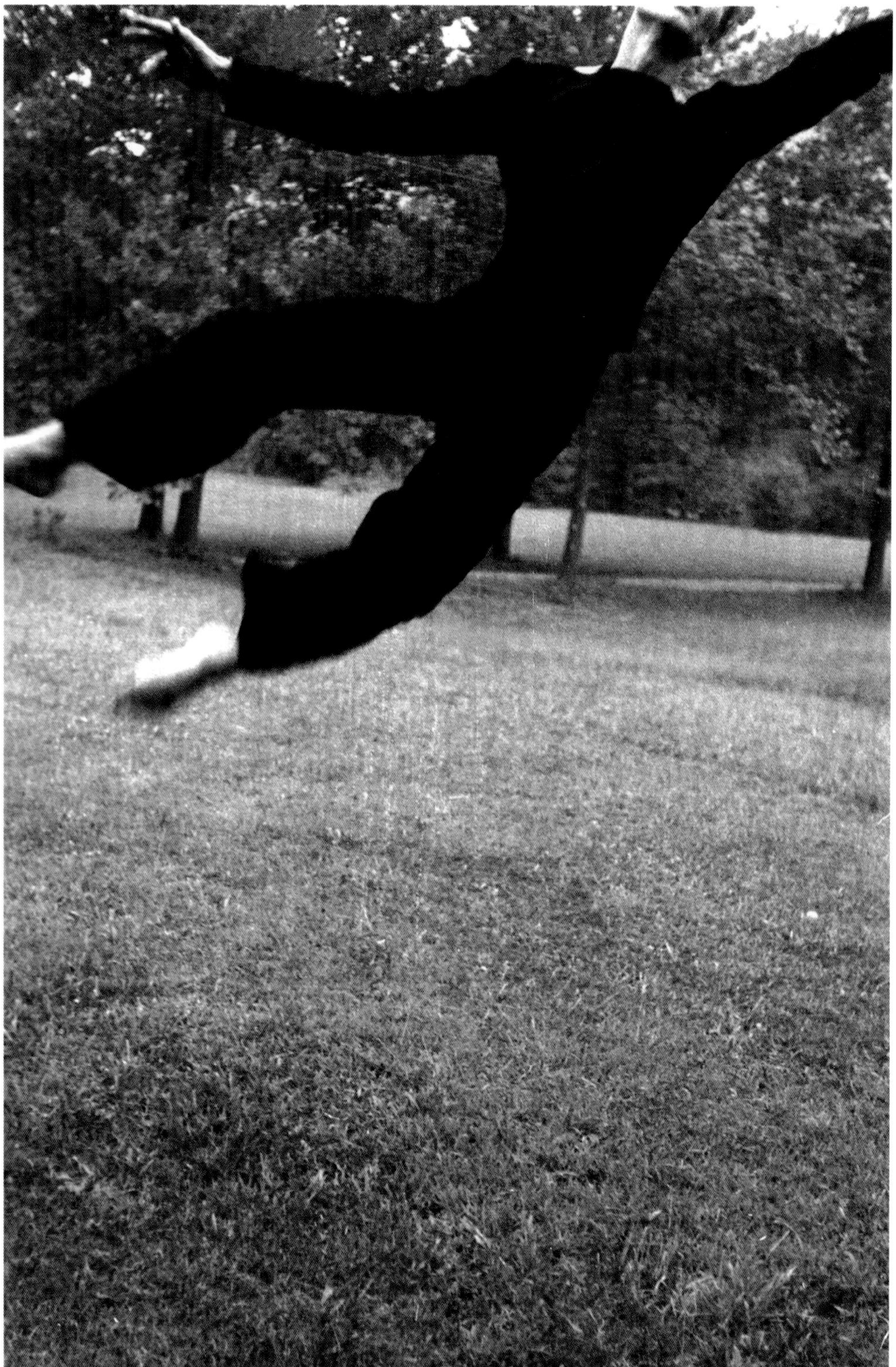

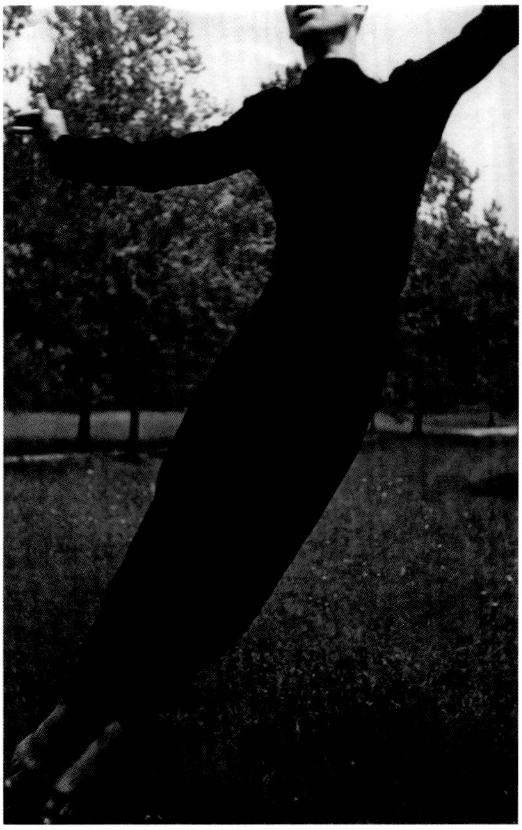

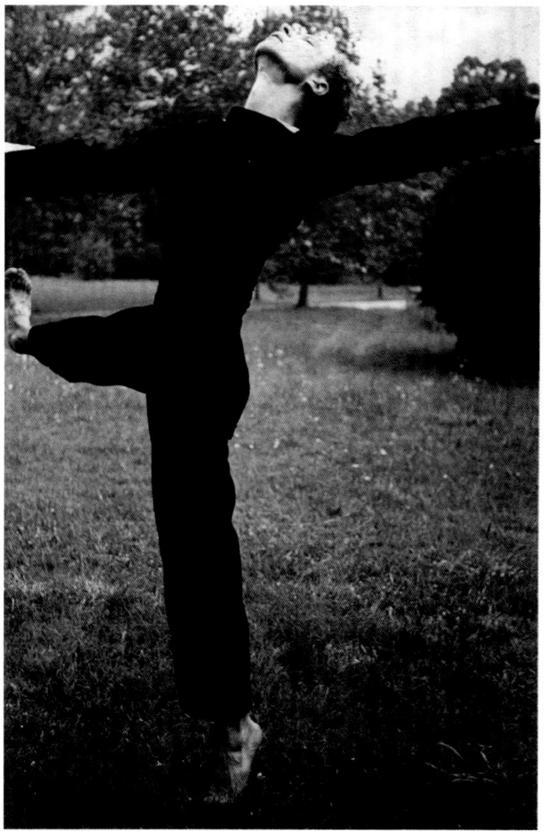

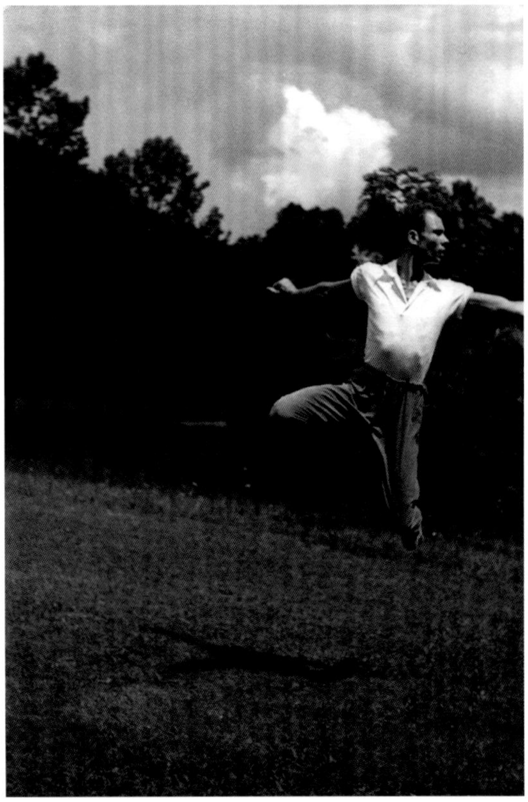 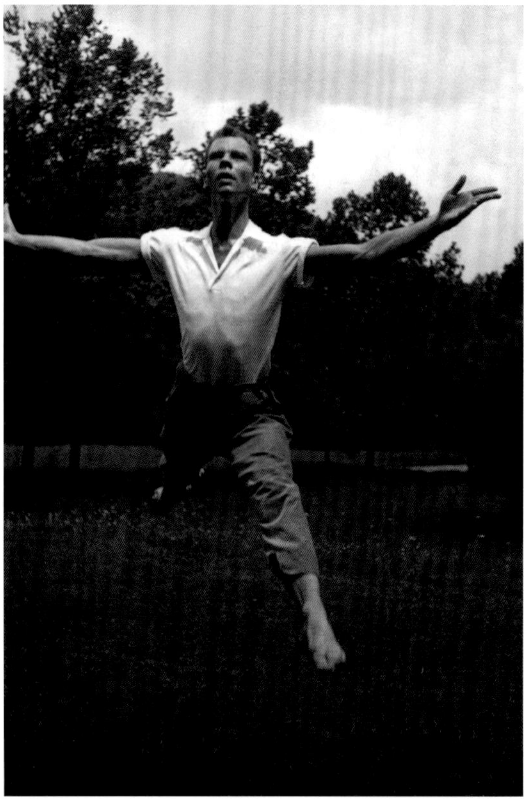

Merce Cunningham

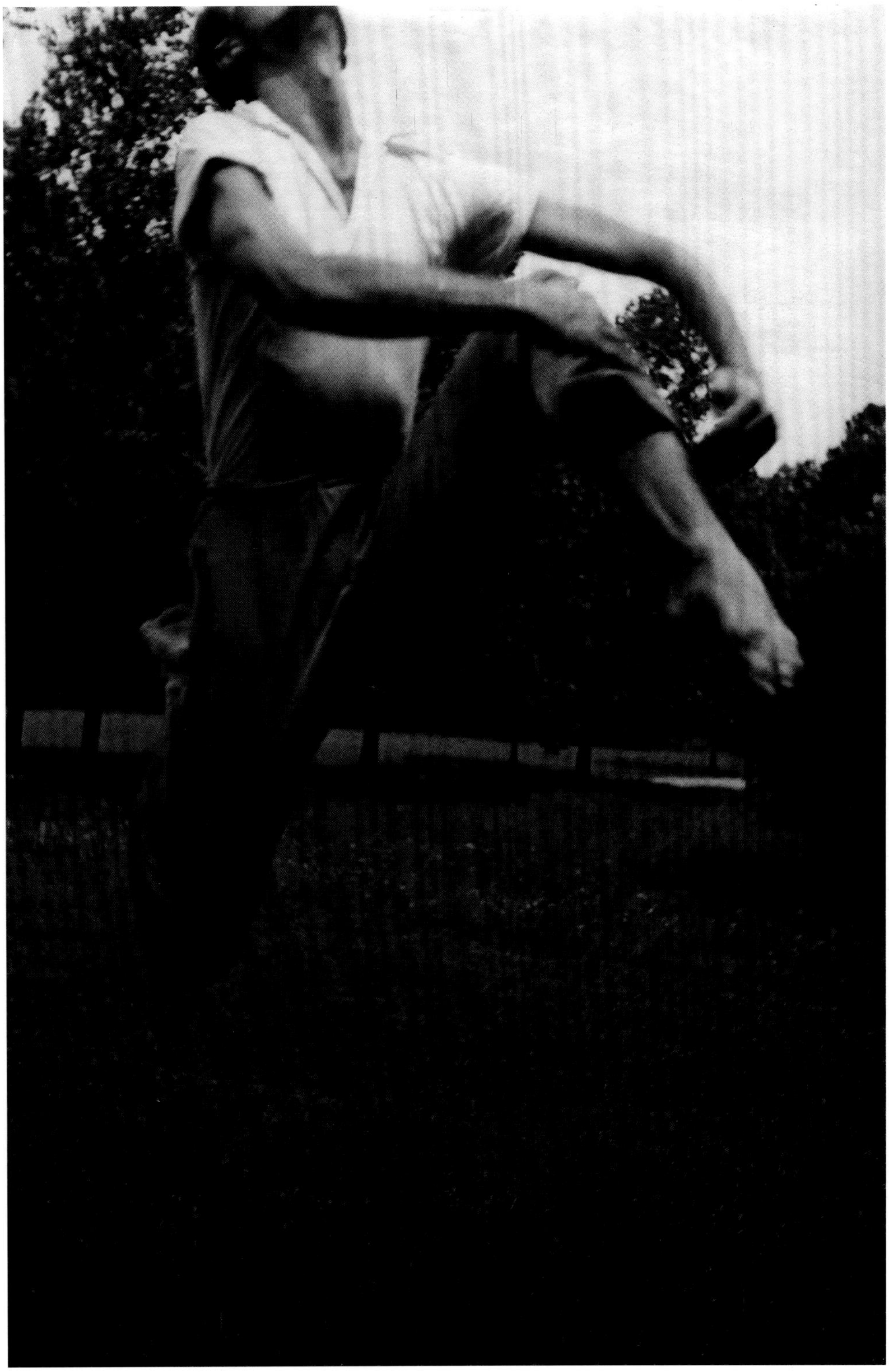

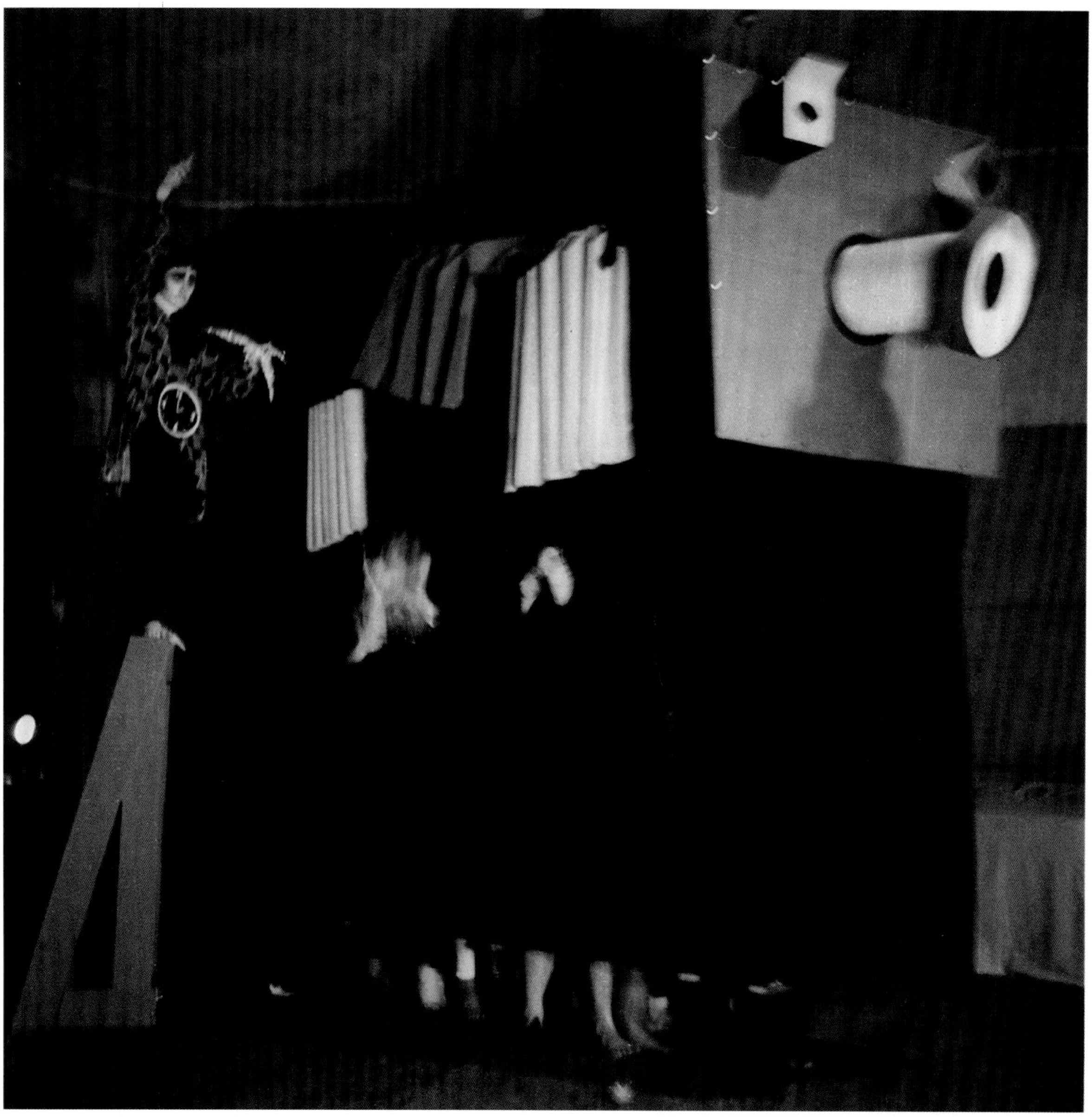

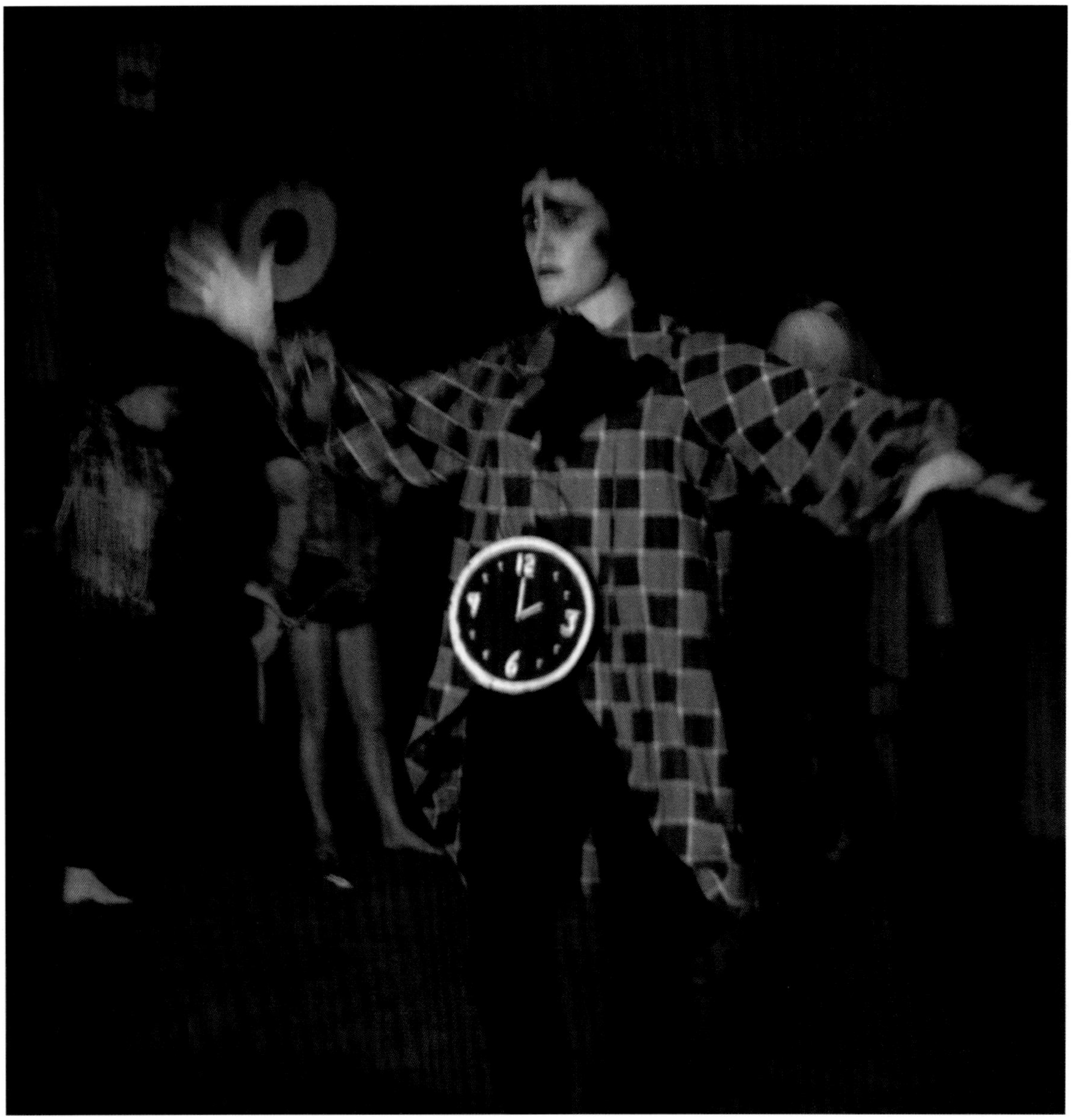

June Rice Christensen as the Photographer in "Marriage on the Eiffel Tower"

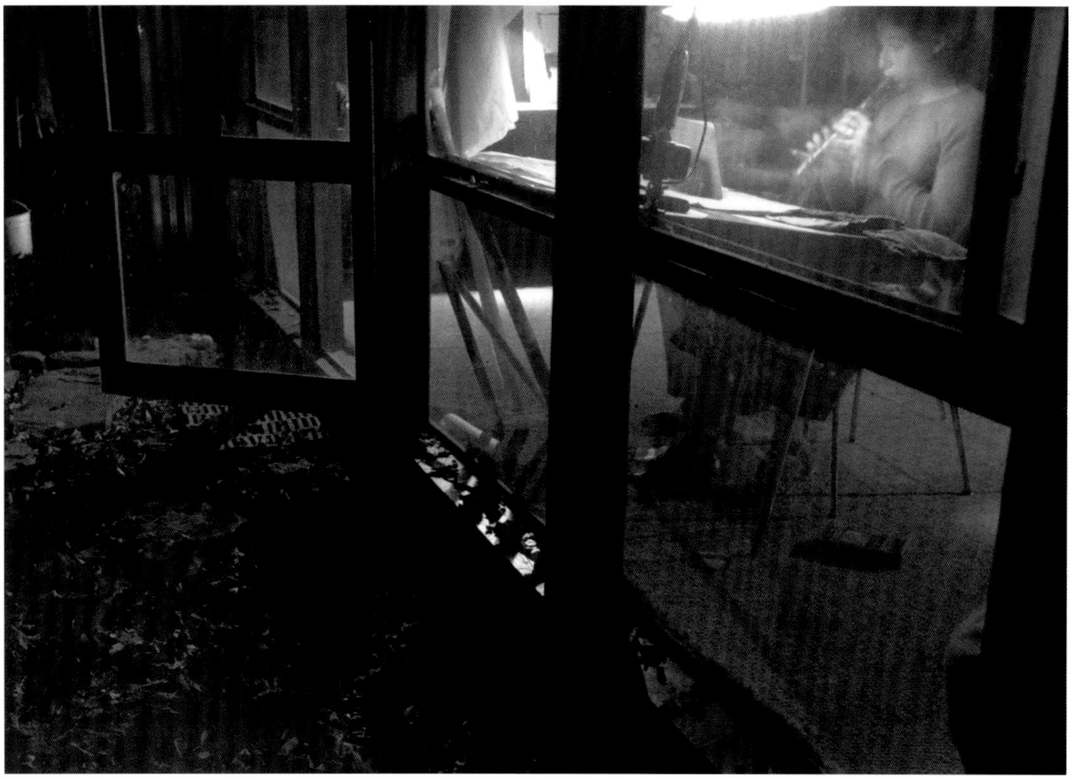

Vera Baker Williams playing the recorder in the Minimum House

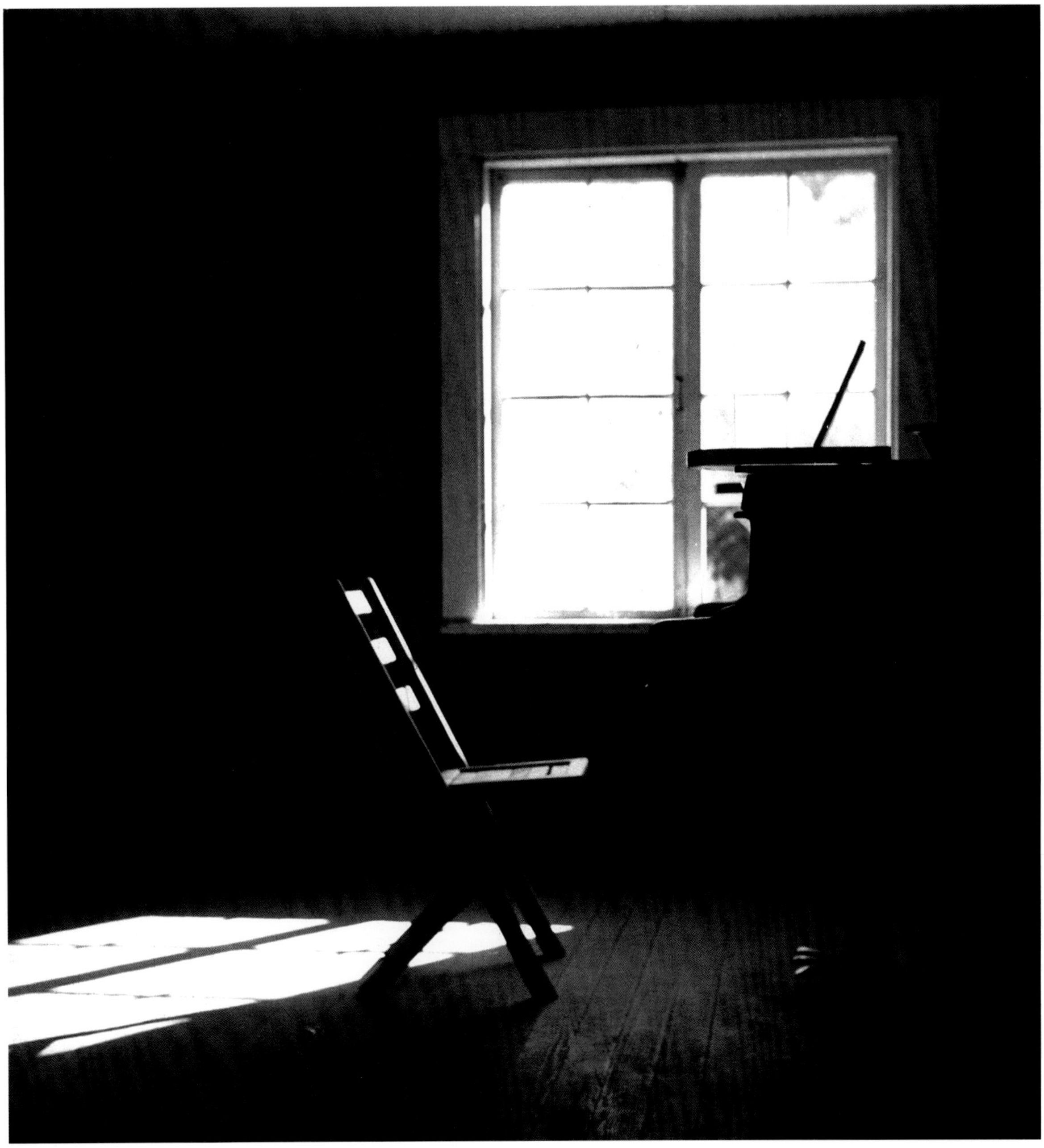

Untitled

# PORTRAITS

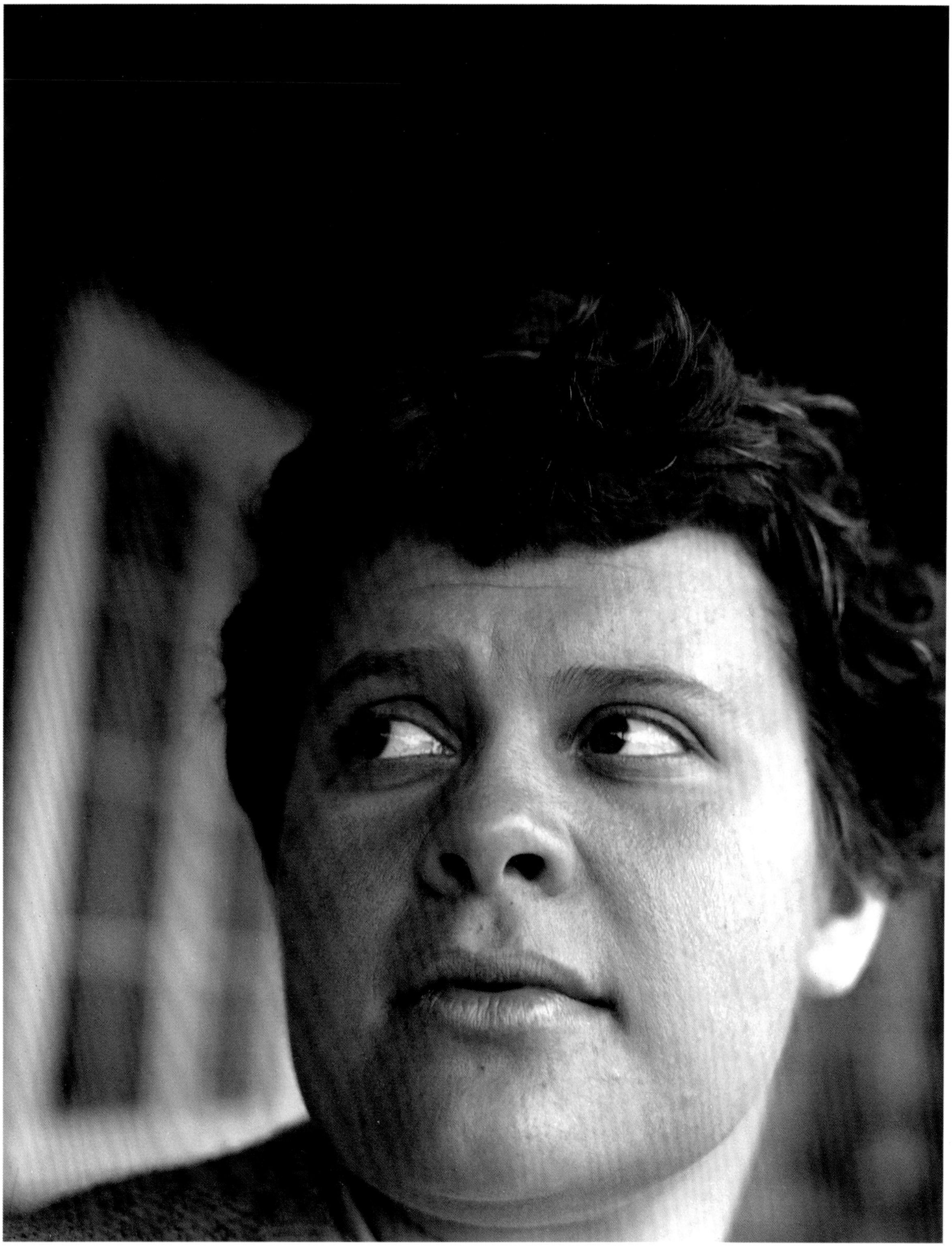

Hazel Larsen Archer

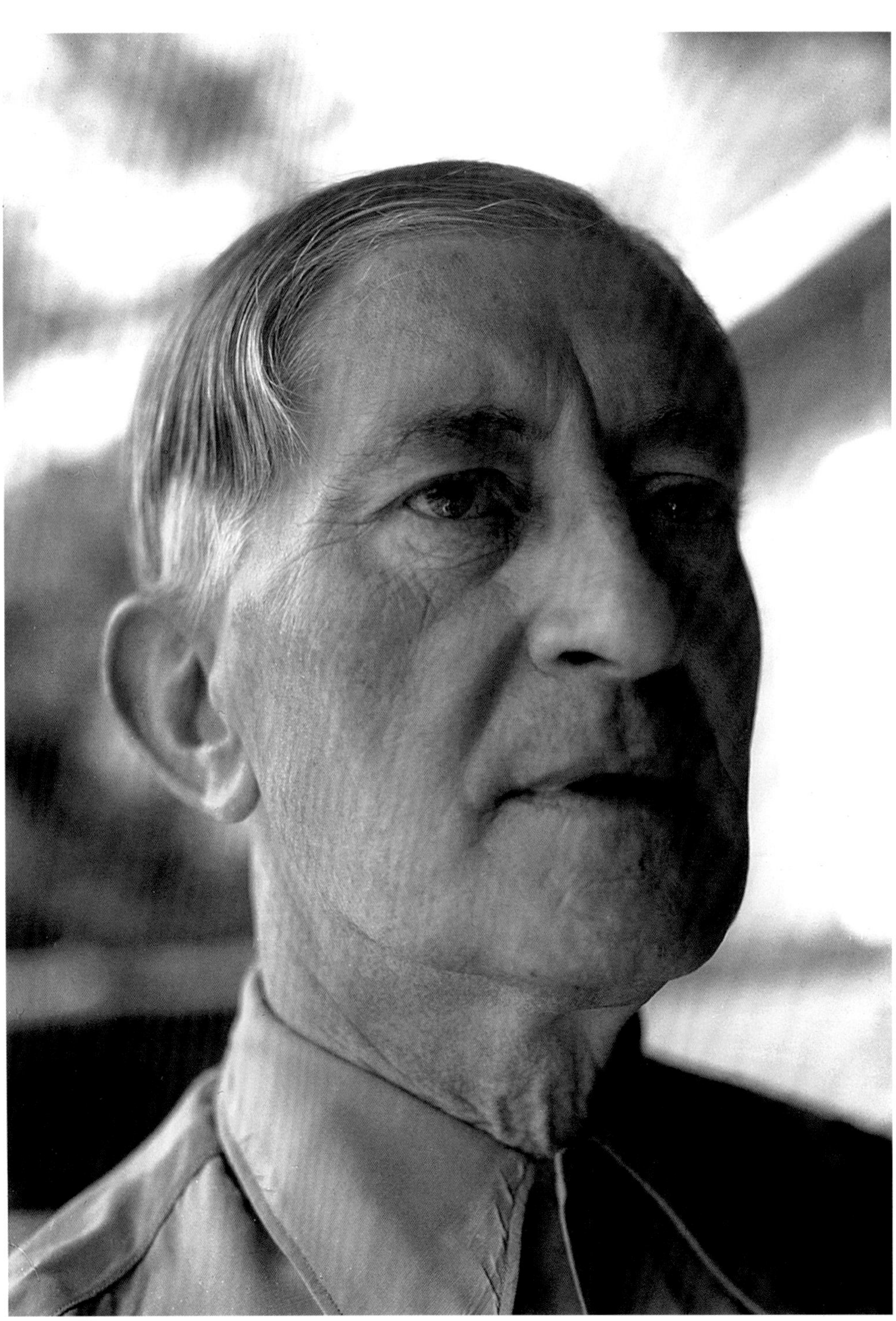

Josef Albers

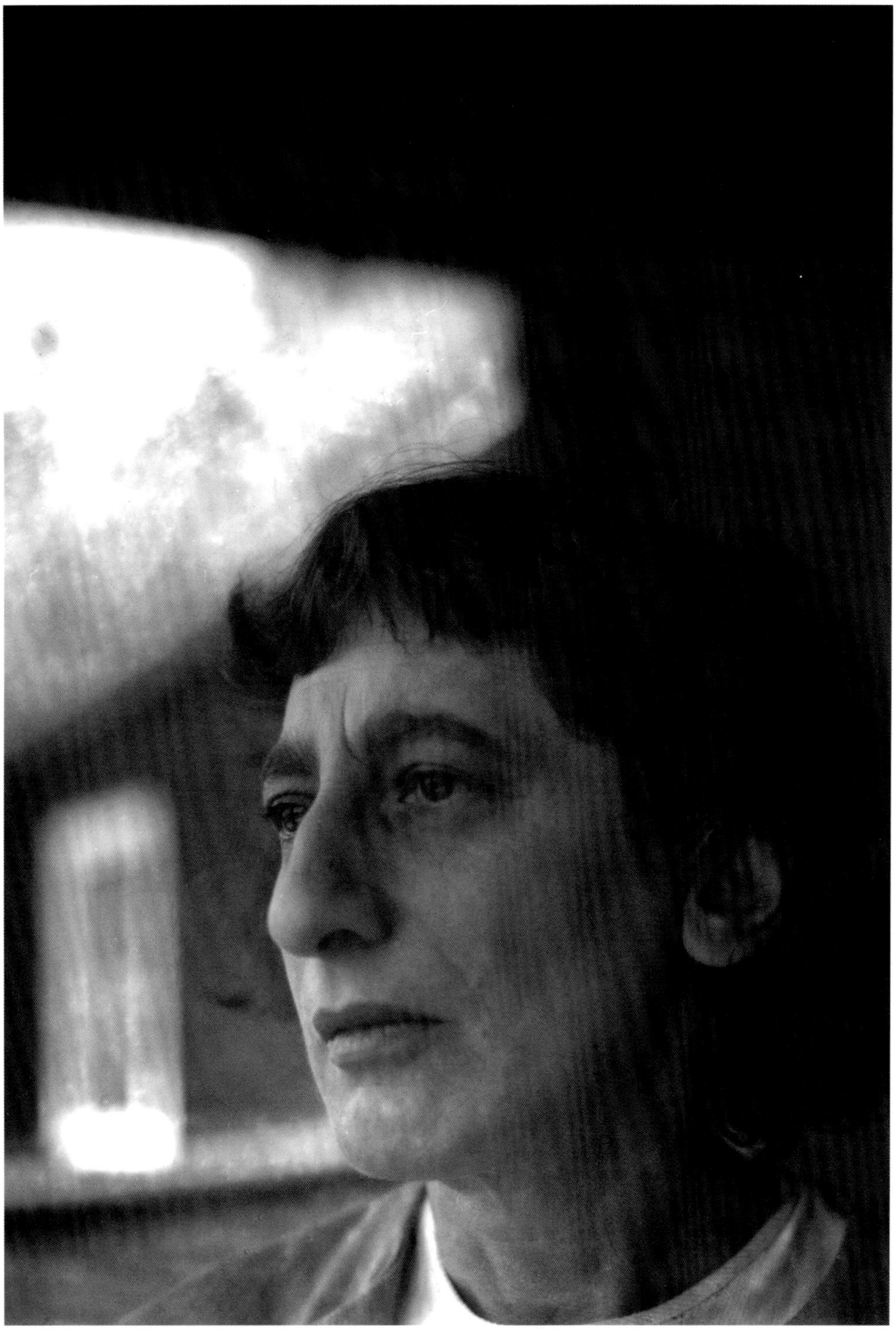

Anni Albers

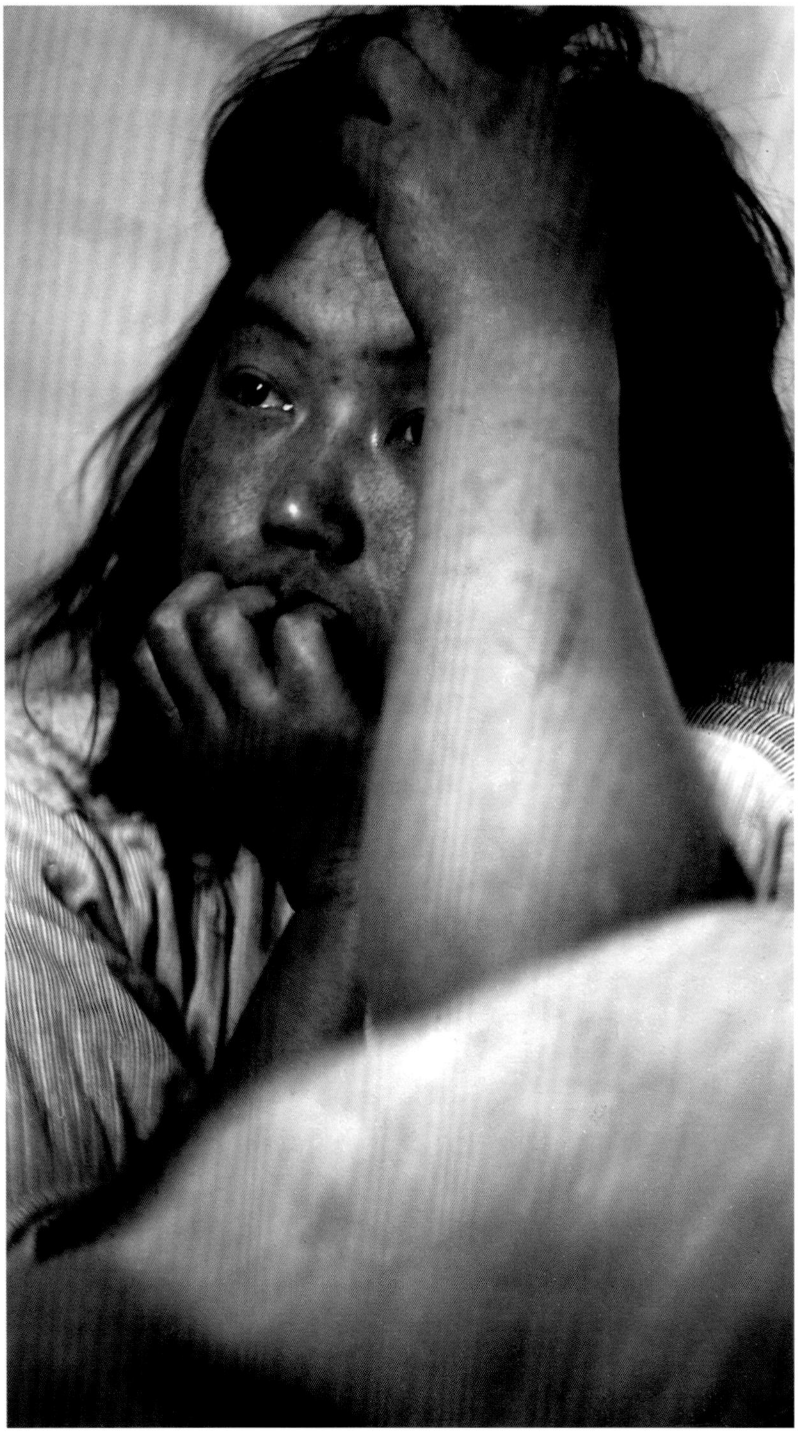

Ruth Asawa

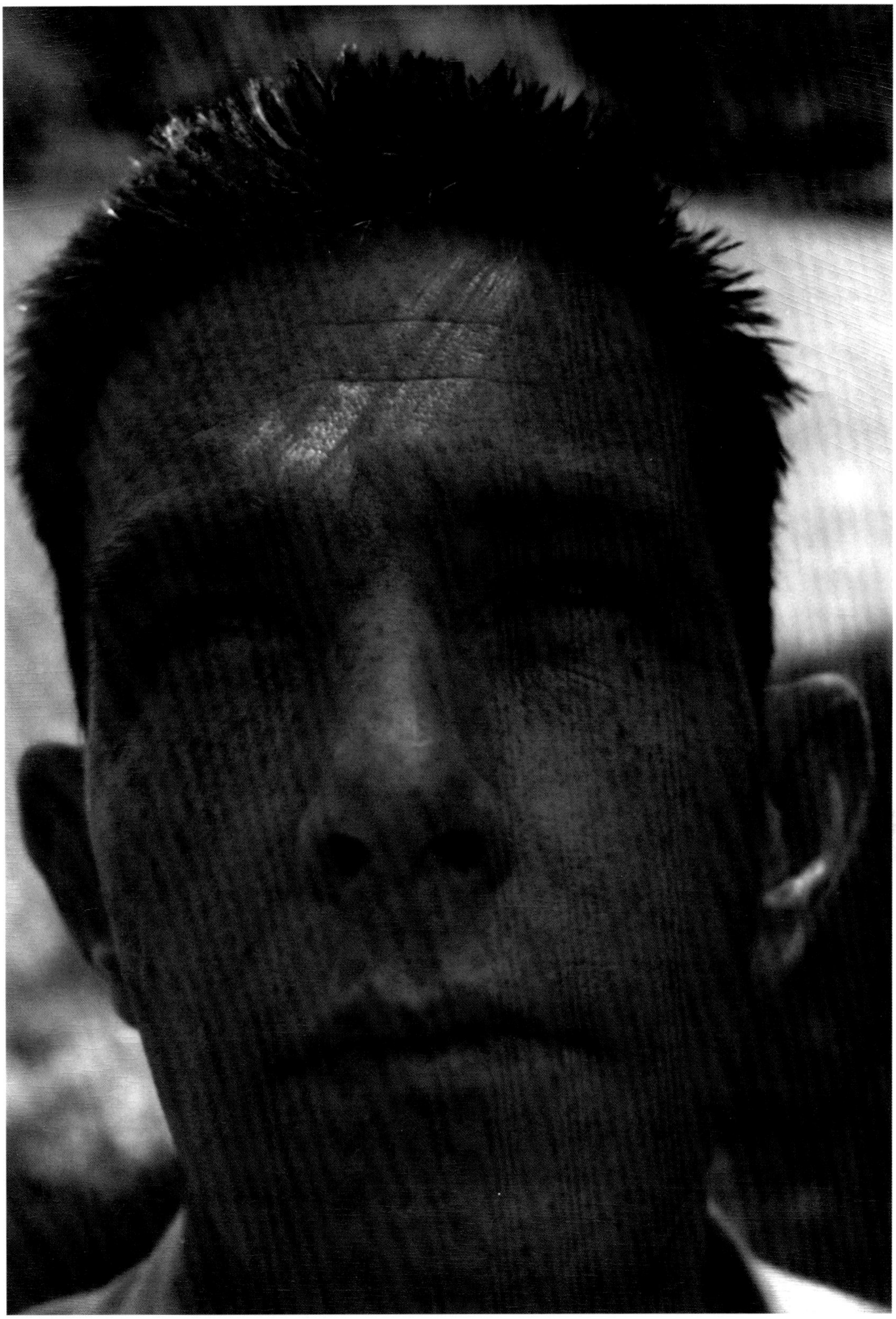

John Cage

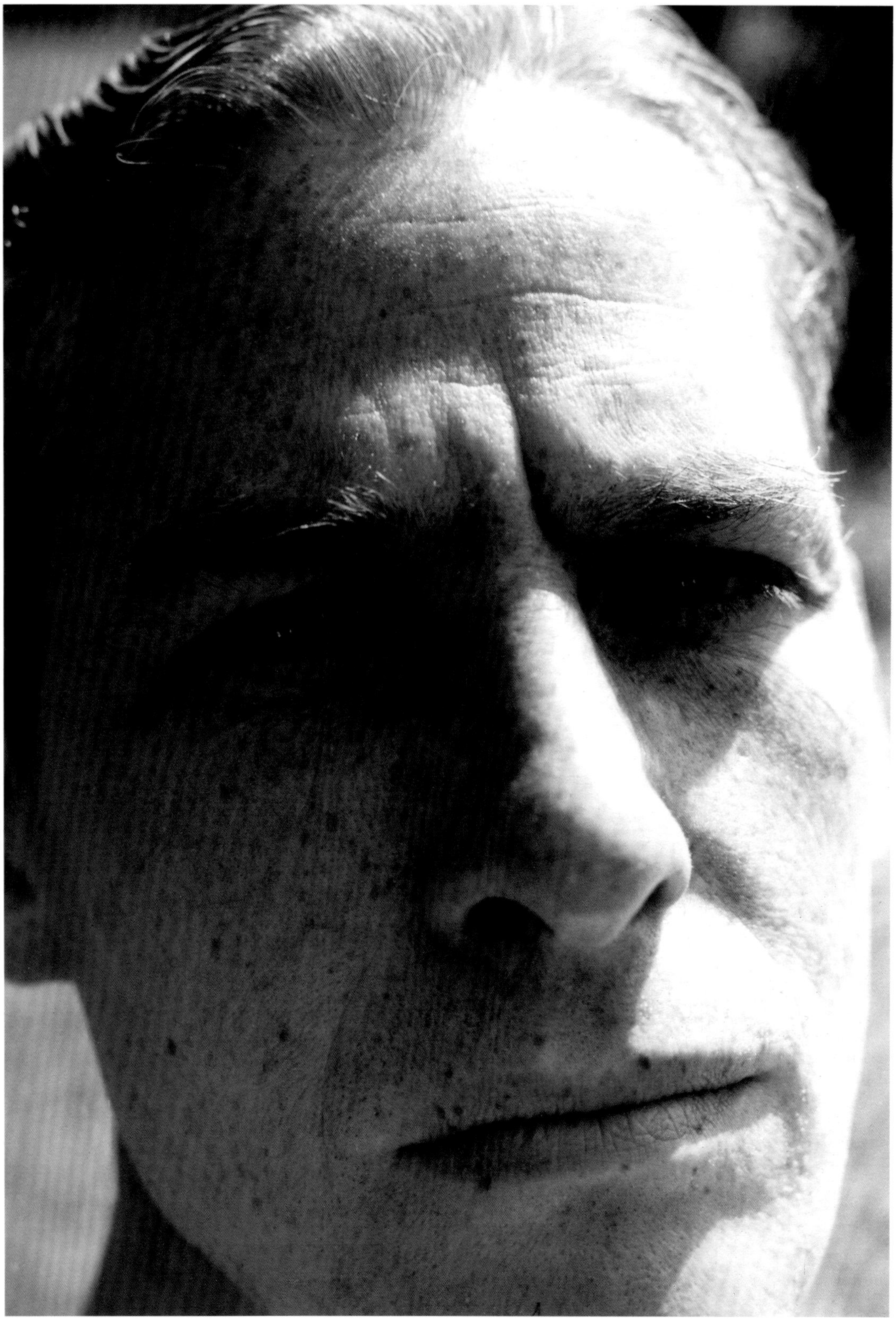

Willem de Kooning

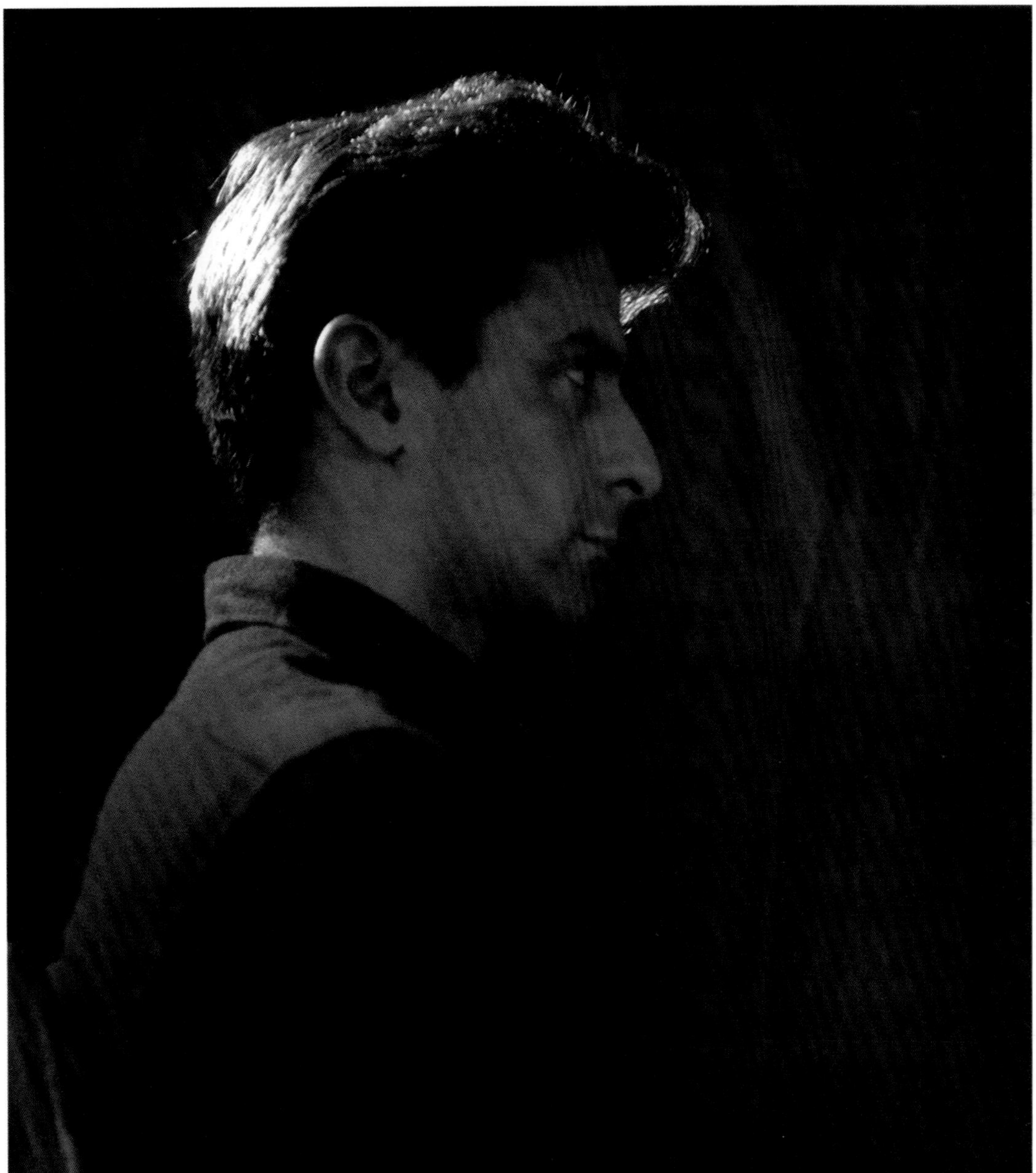

Joseph Fiore

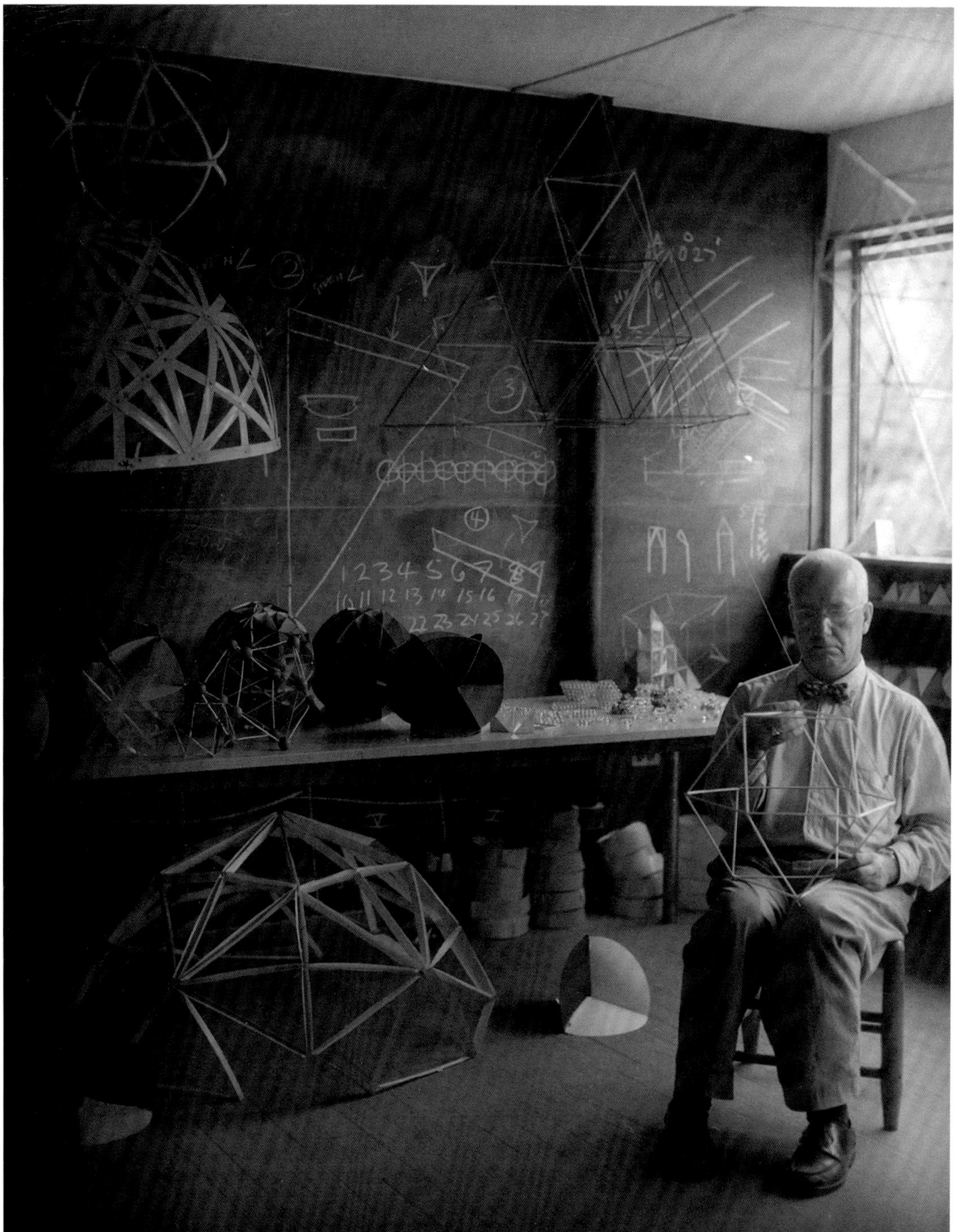

Buckminster Fuller

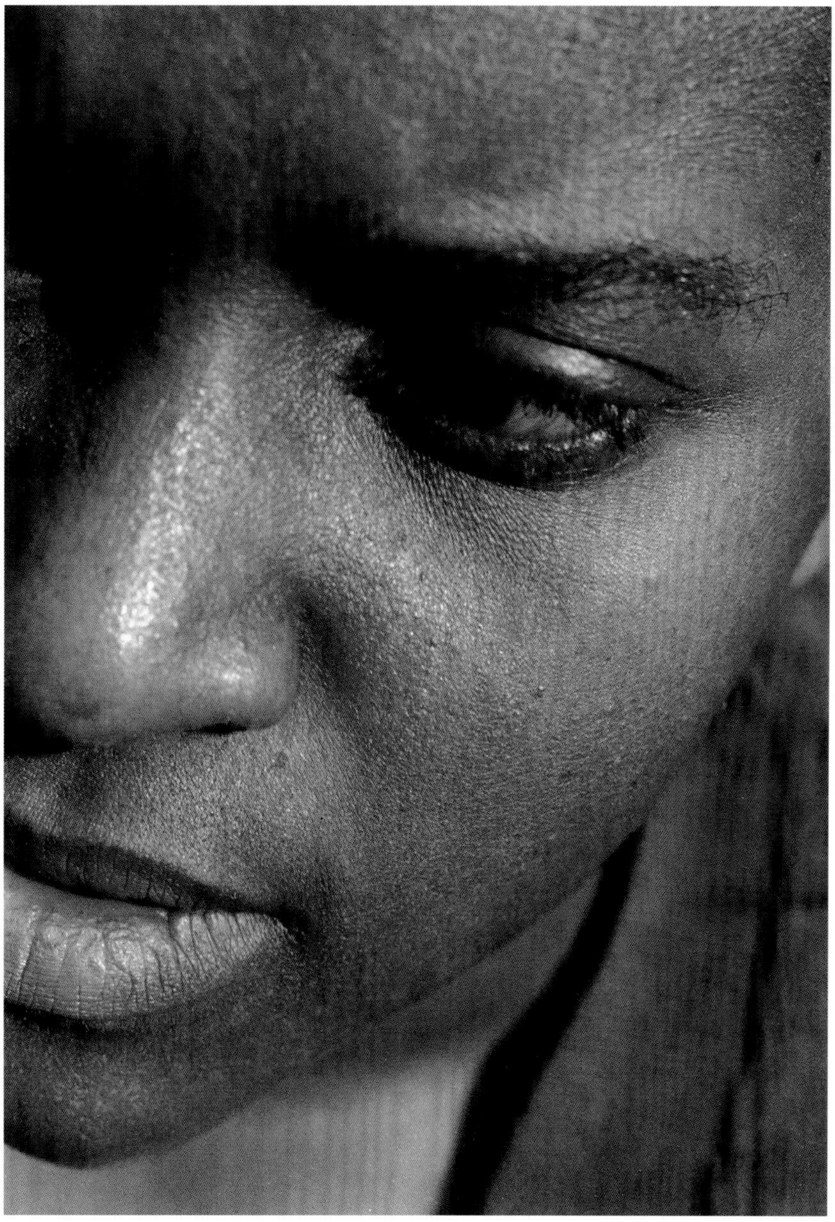

Delores Fullman

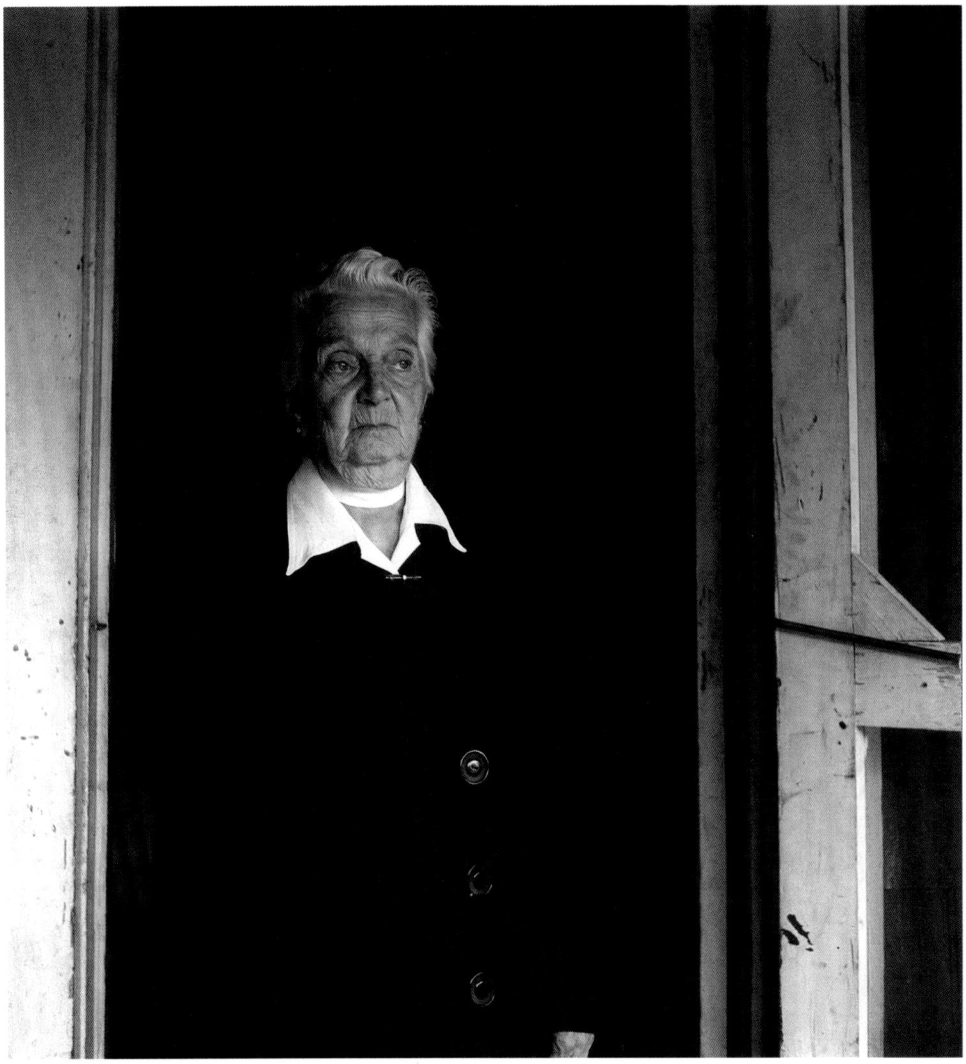

Madame Anna Goldowski

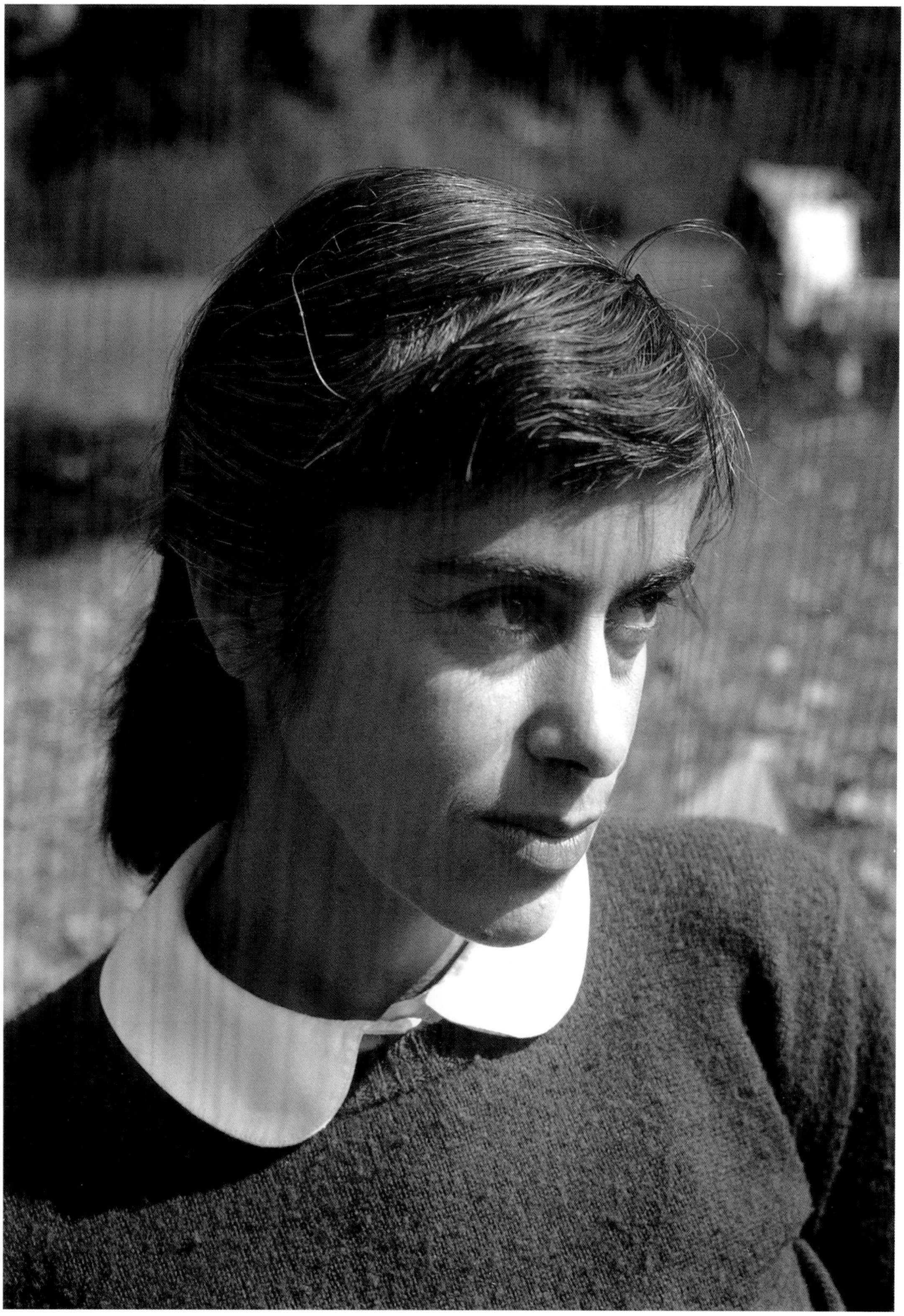

Trude Guermonprez

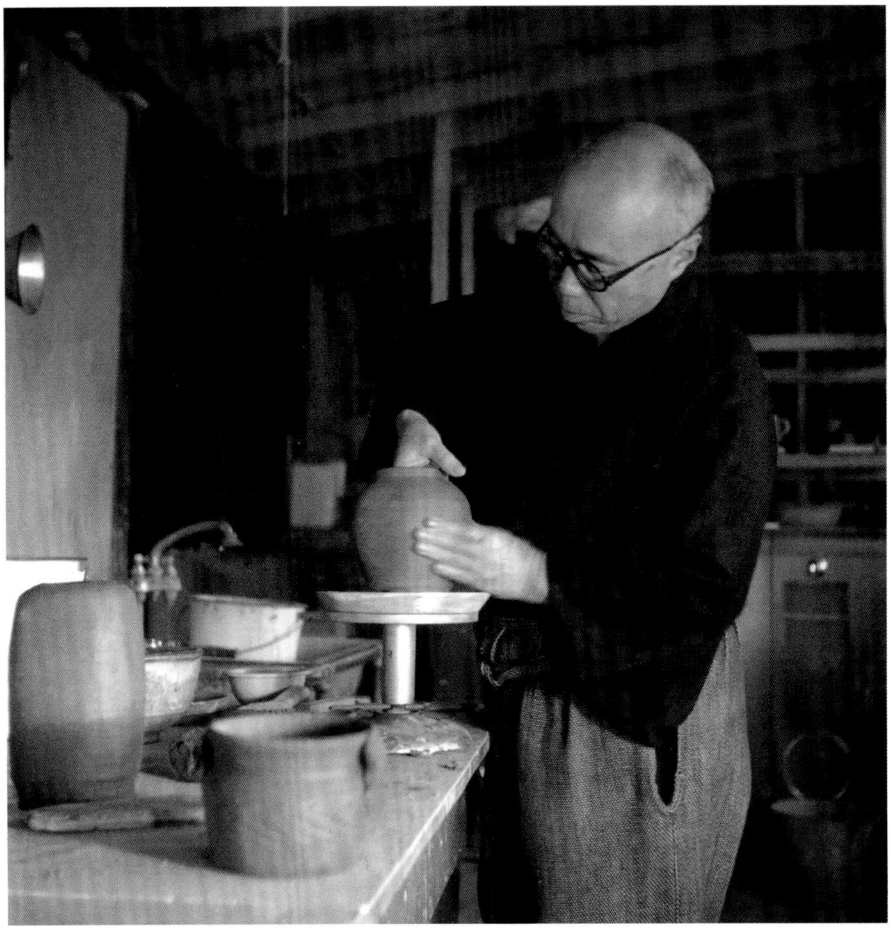

Shoji Hamada, 1952

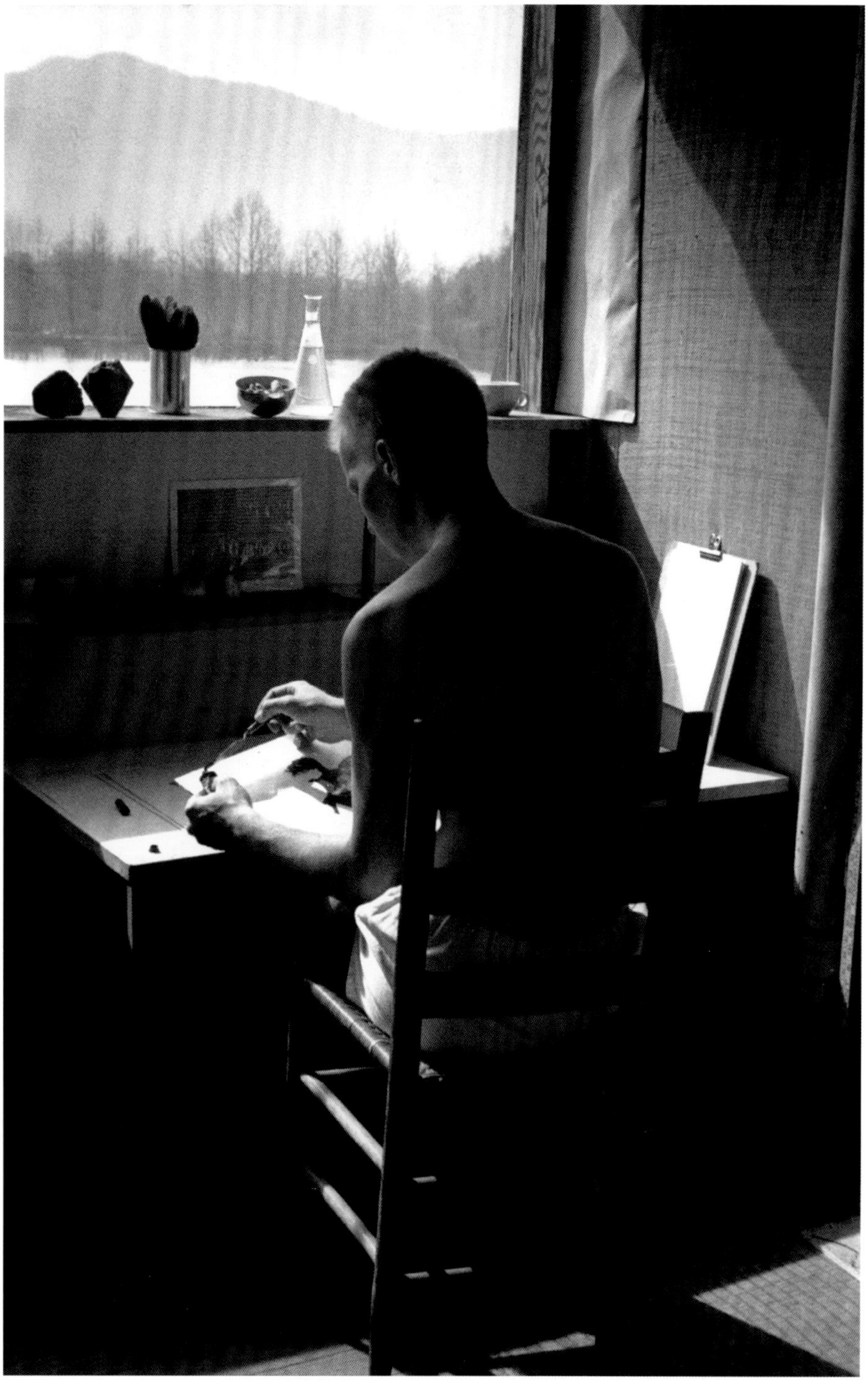

Ray Johnson

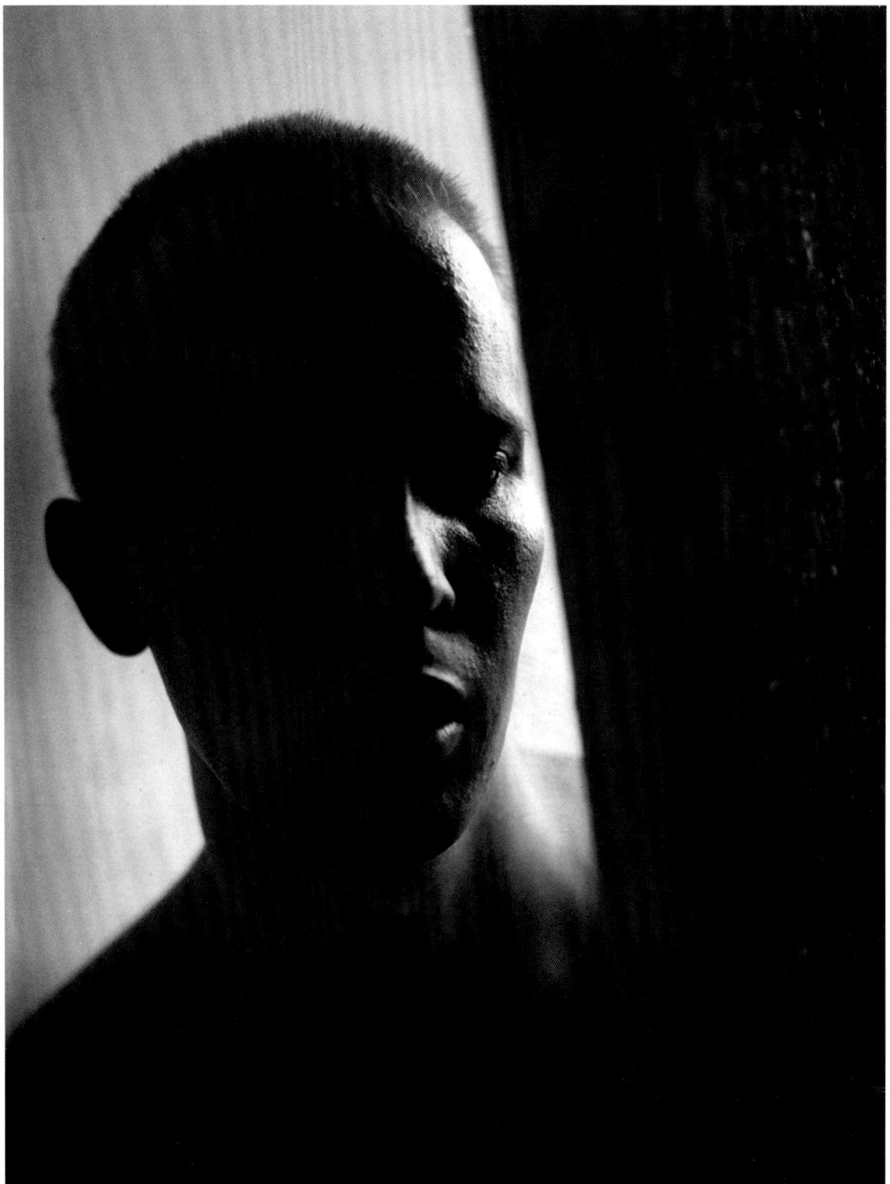

Ray Johnson

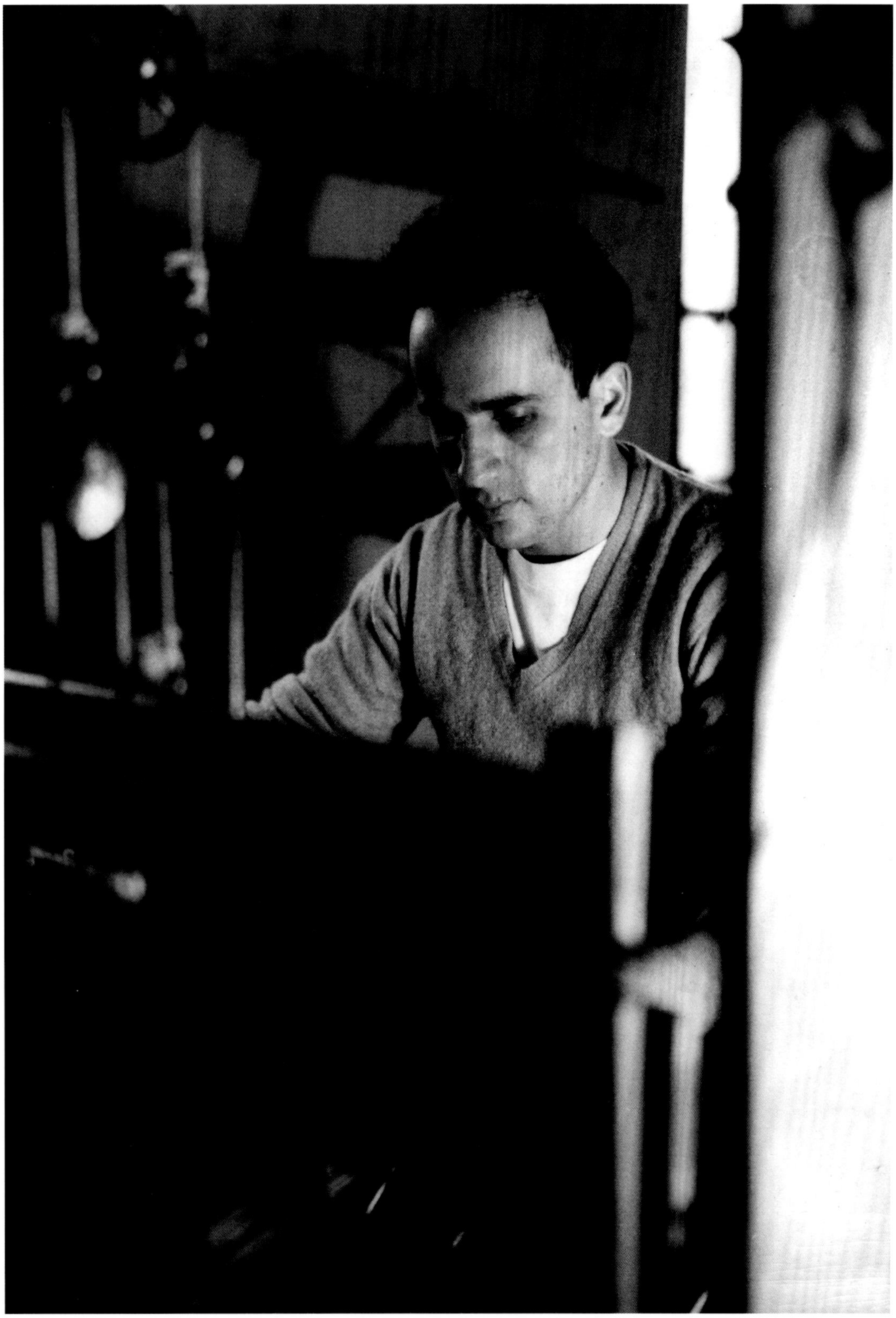

William Joseph

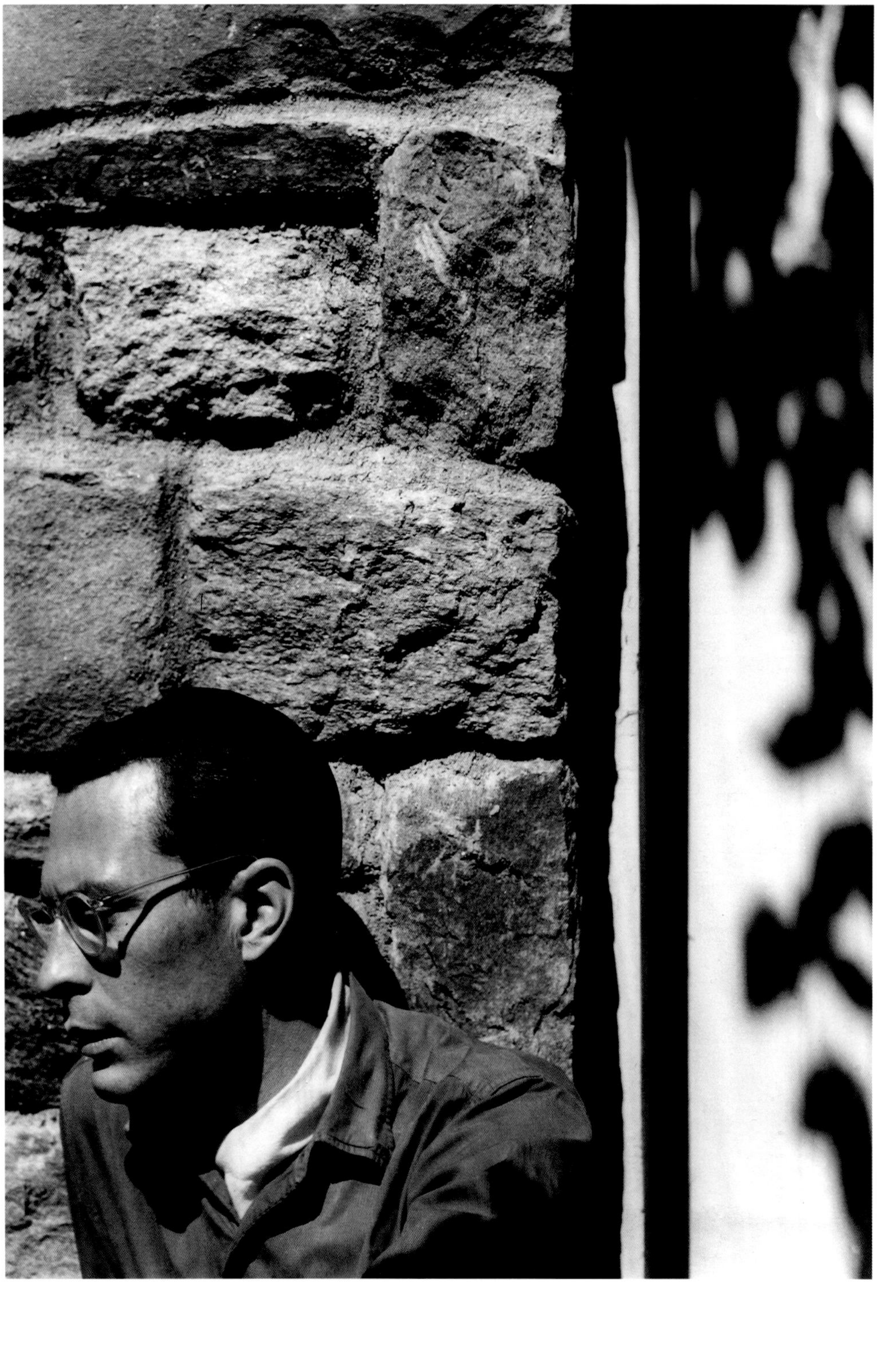

Nick Muzenic

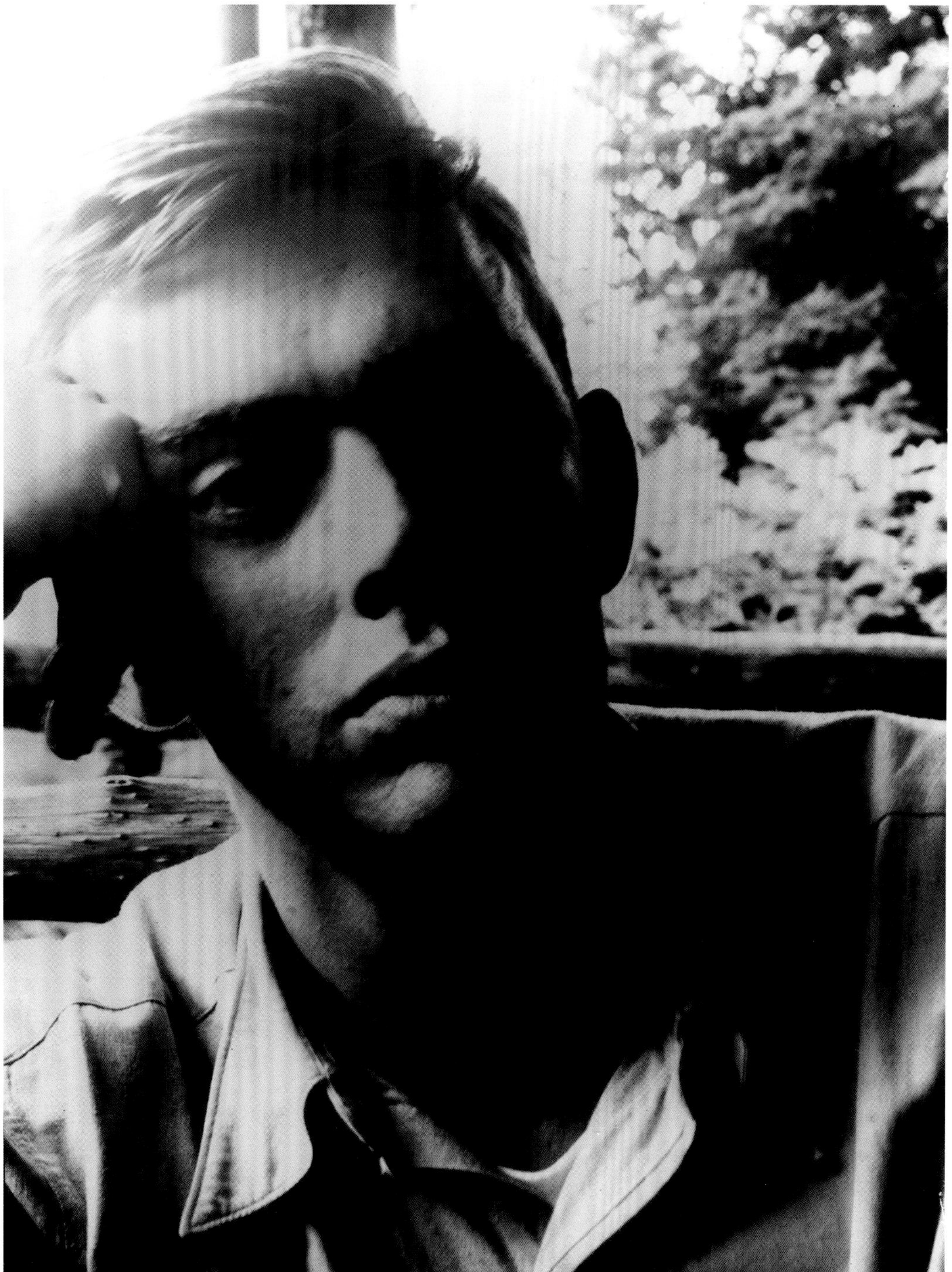

Andrew Oates

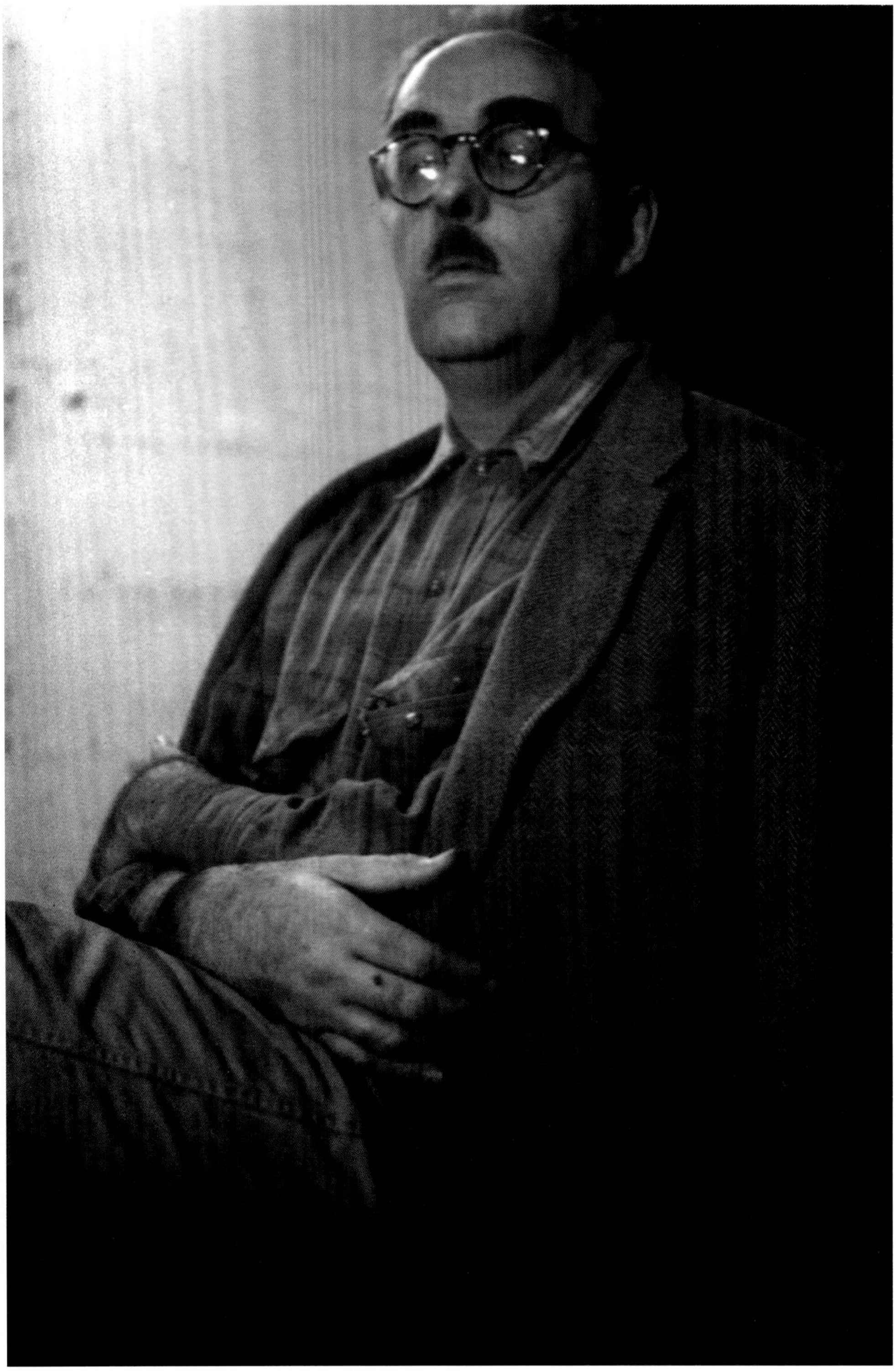

Charles Olson

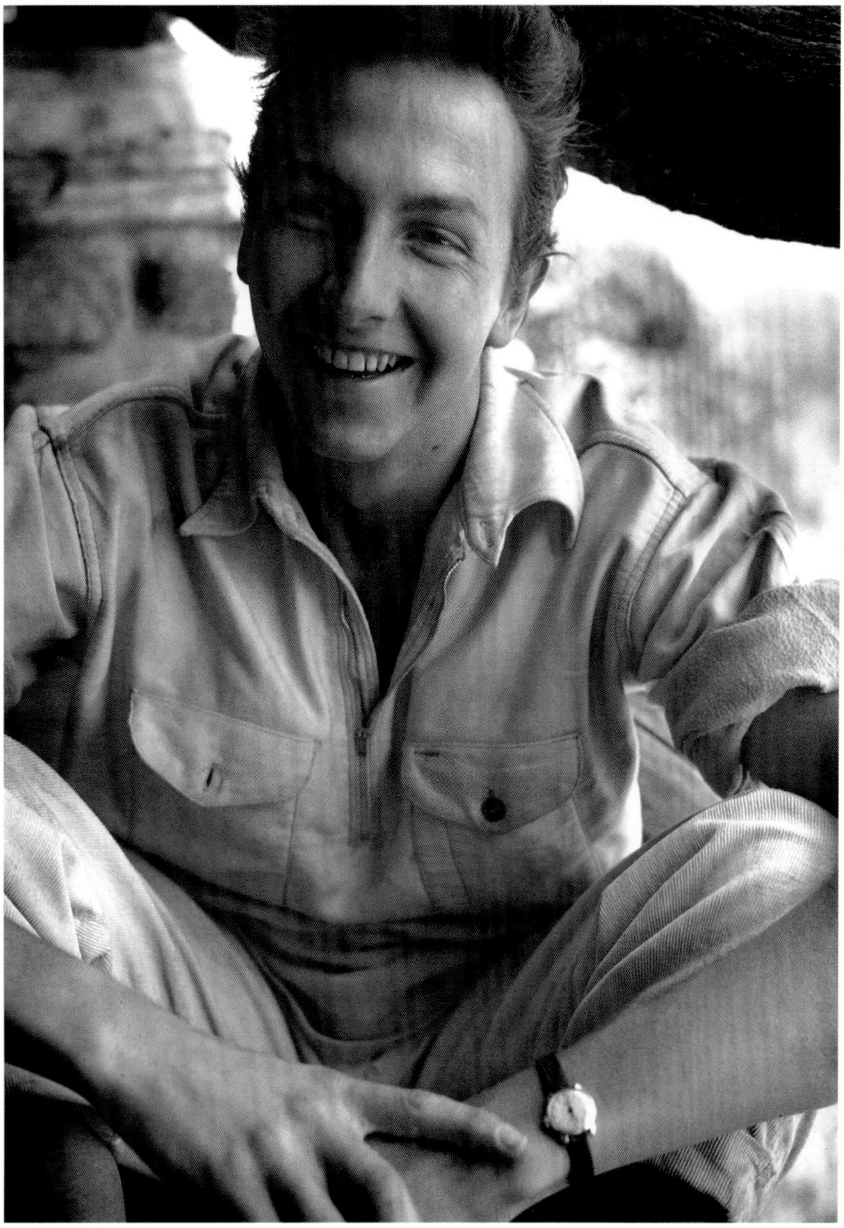

Robert Rauschenberg

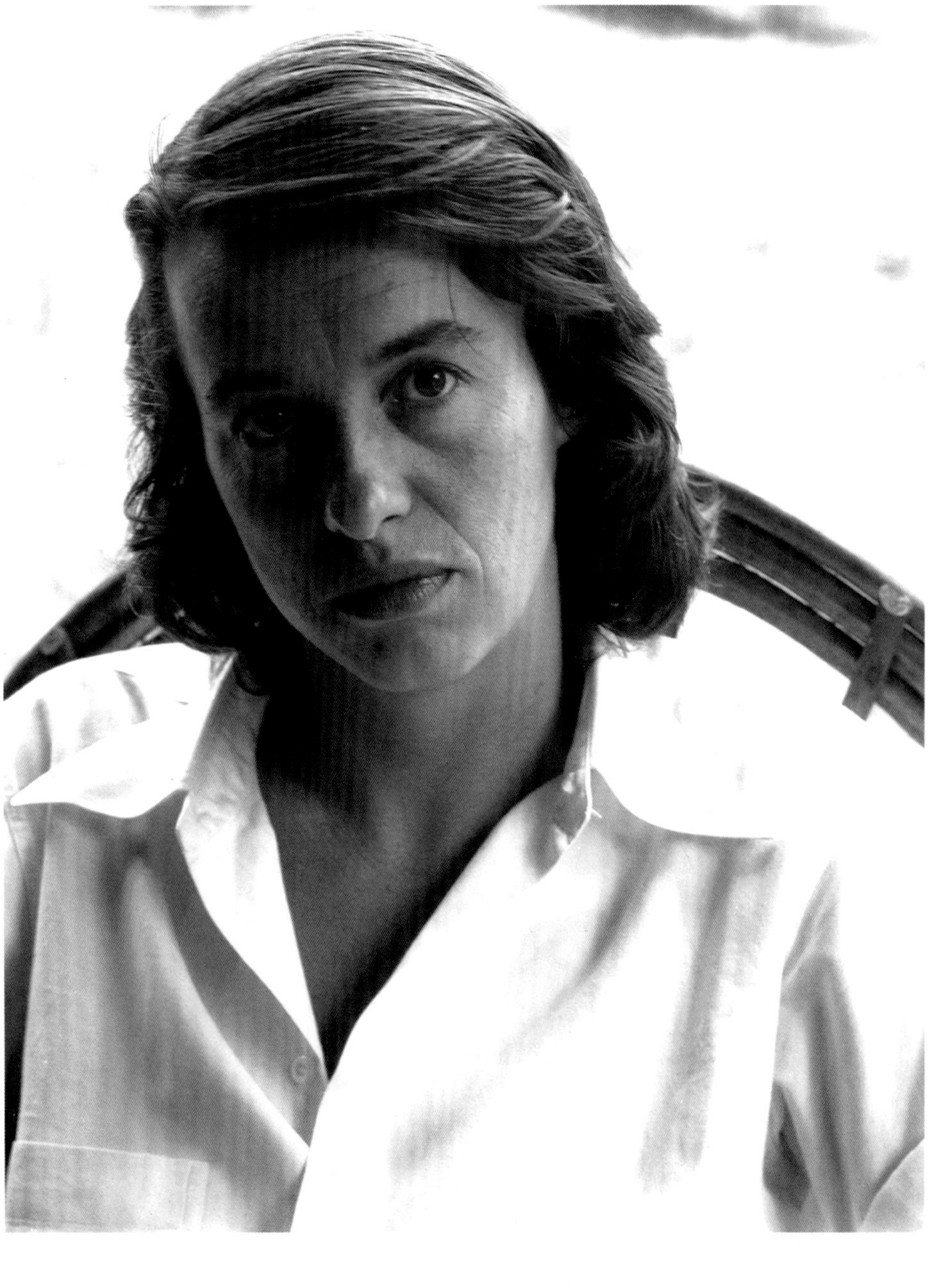

M.C. Richards

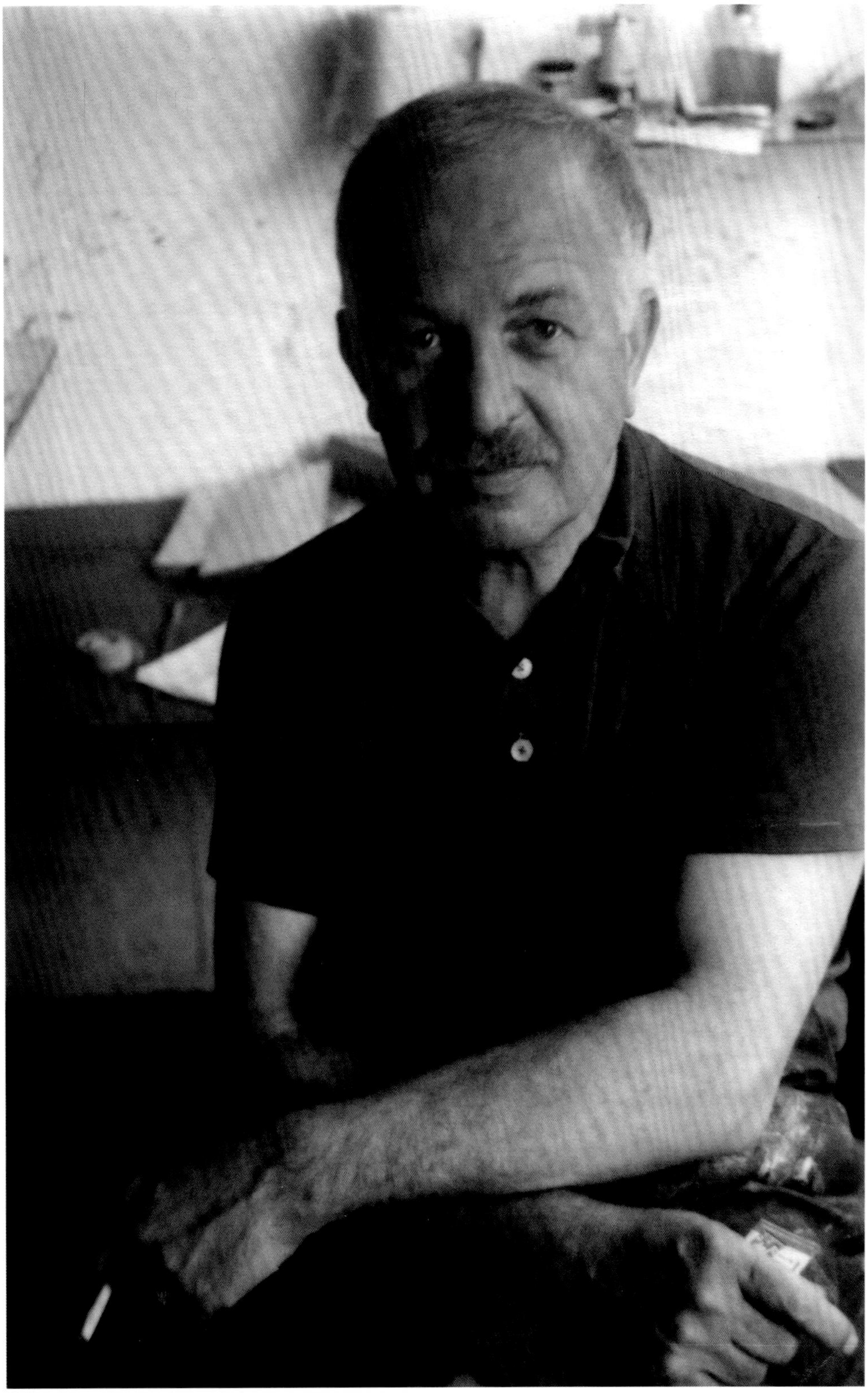

Ben Shahn

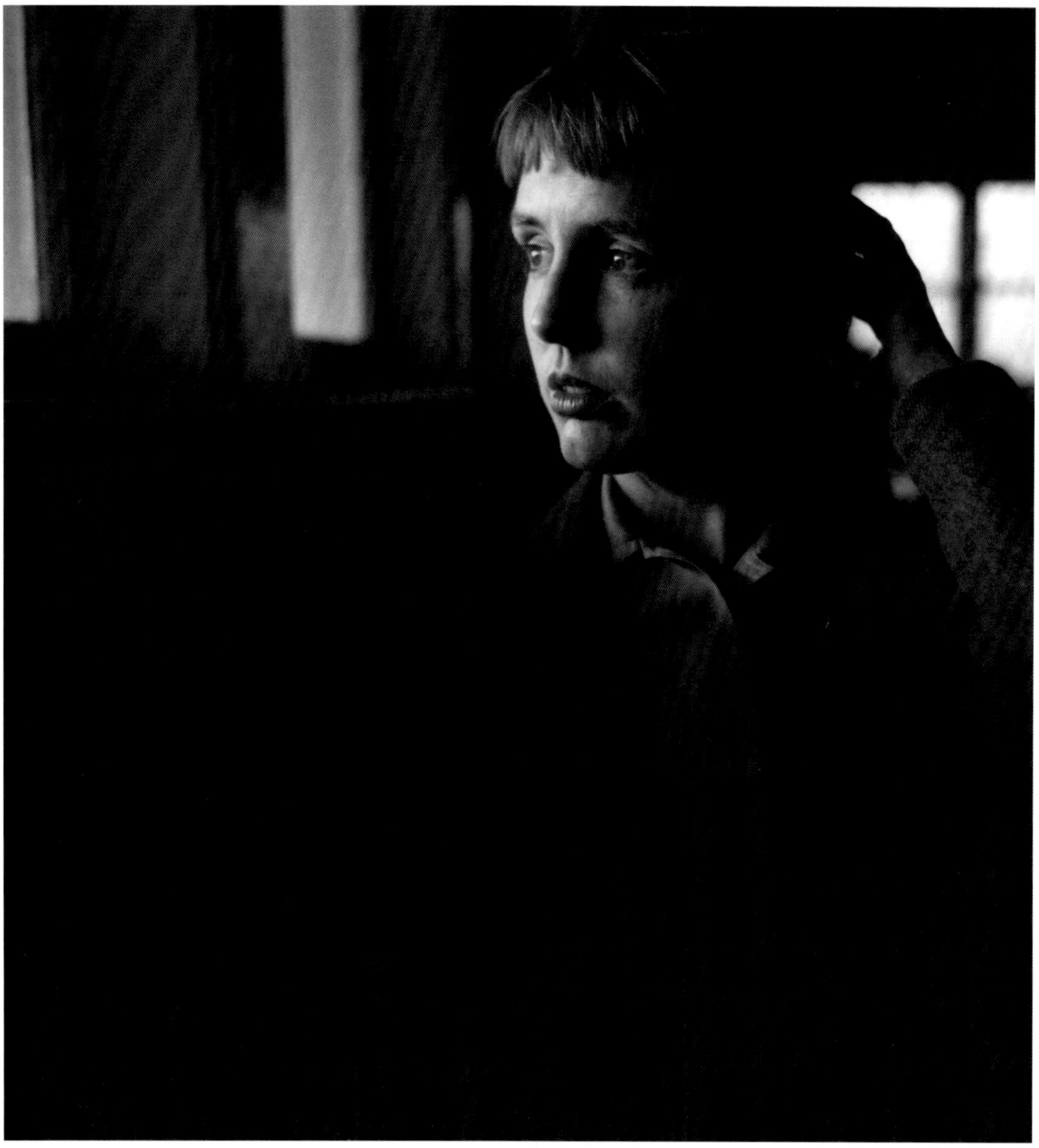

Joan Stack

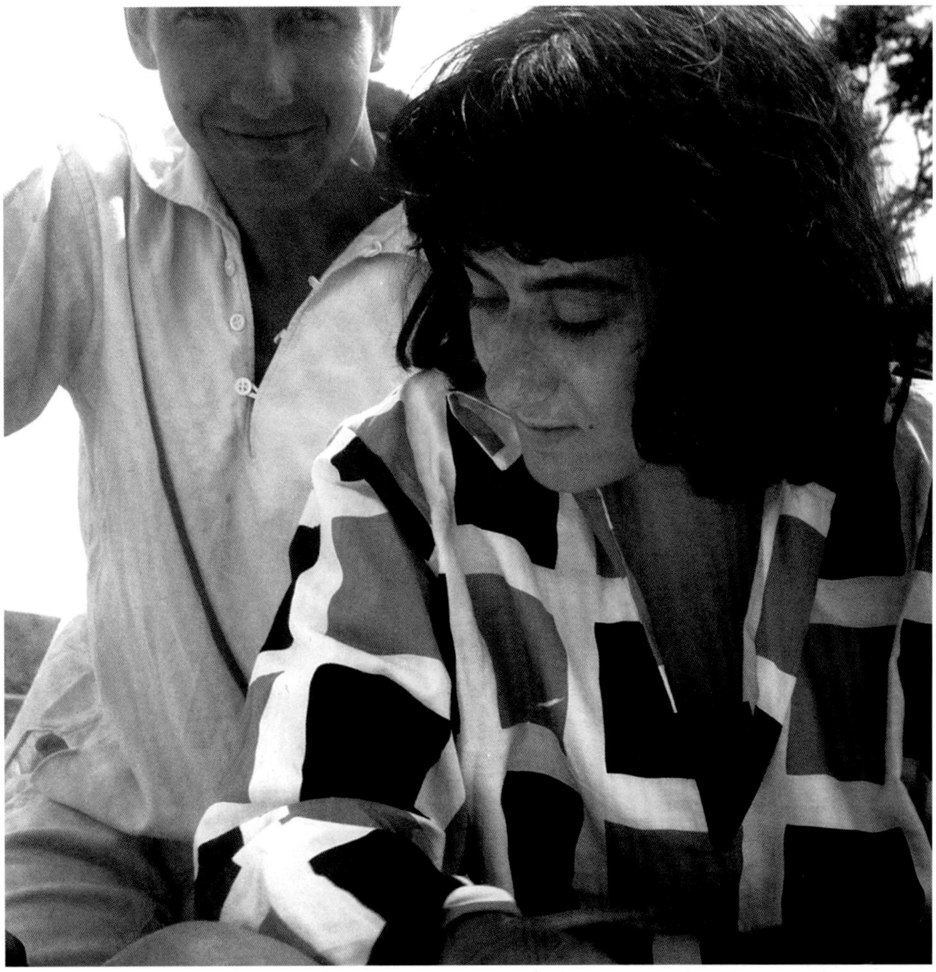

Sue Weil with Robert Rauschenberg

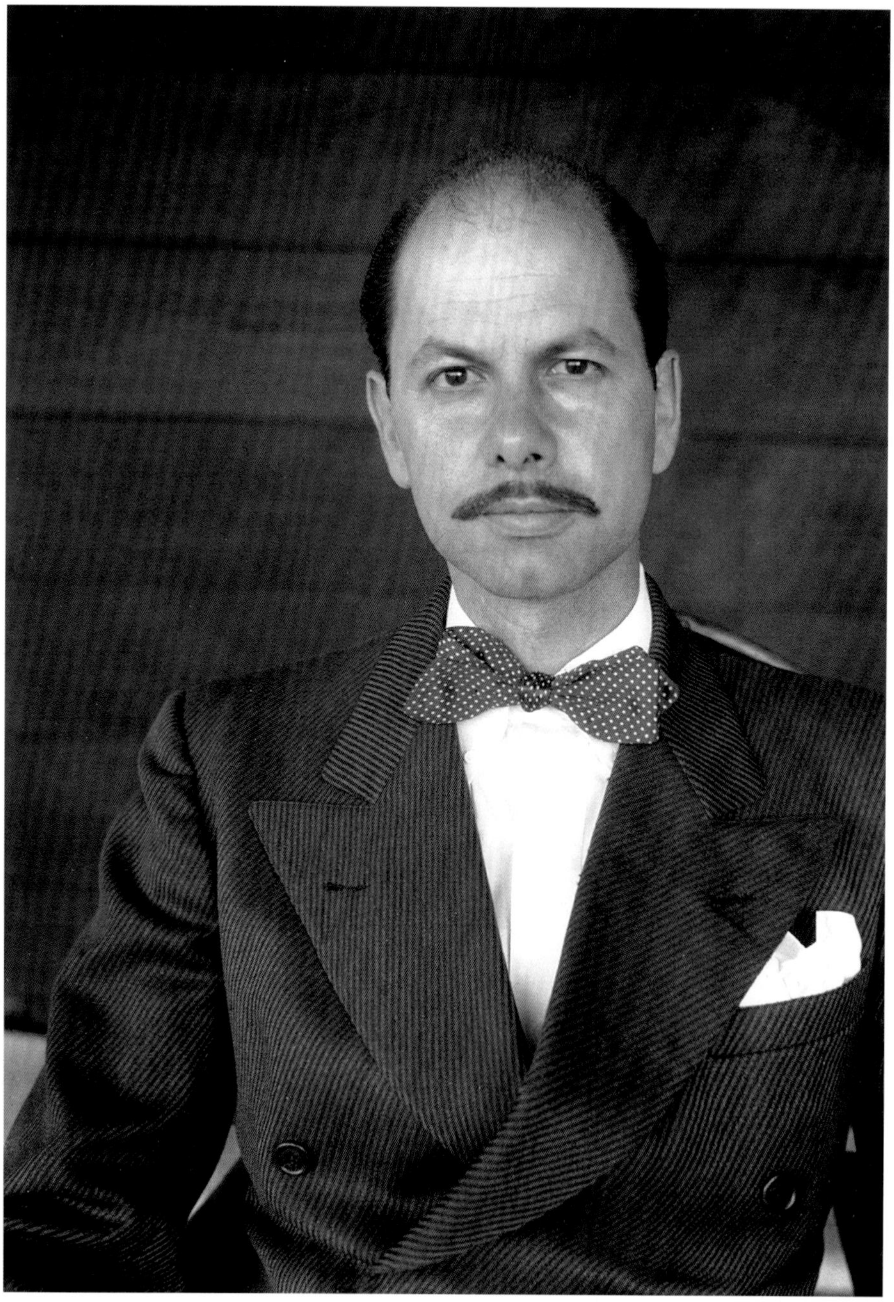

Albert Williams Levi

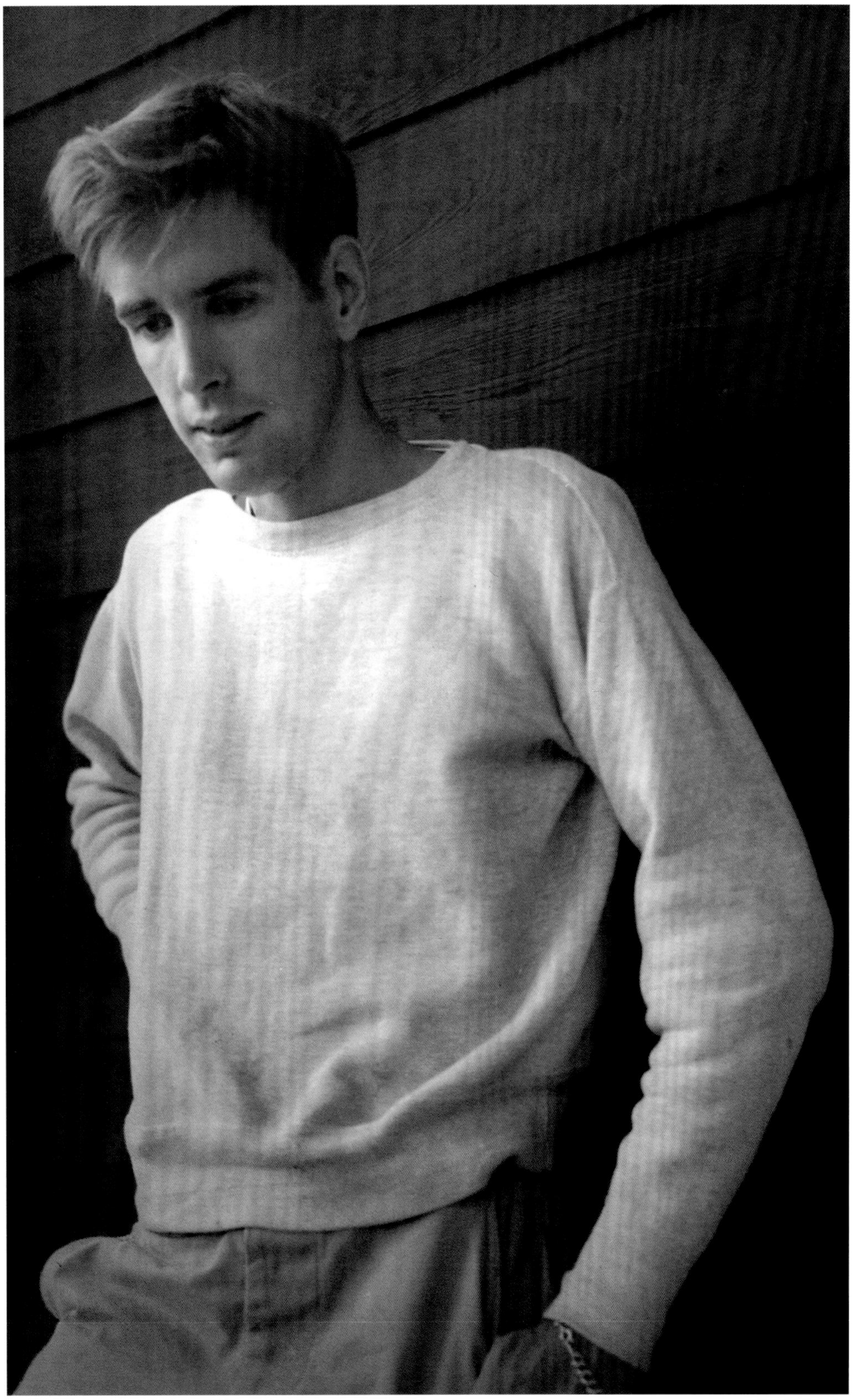

Paul Williams

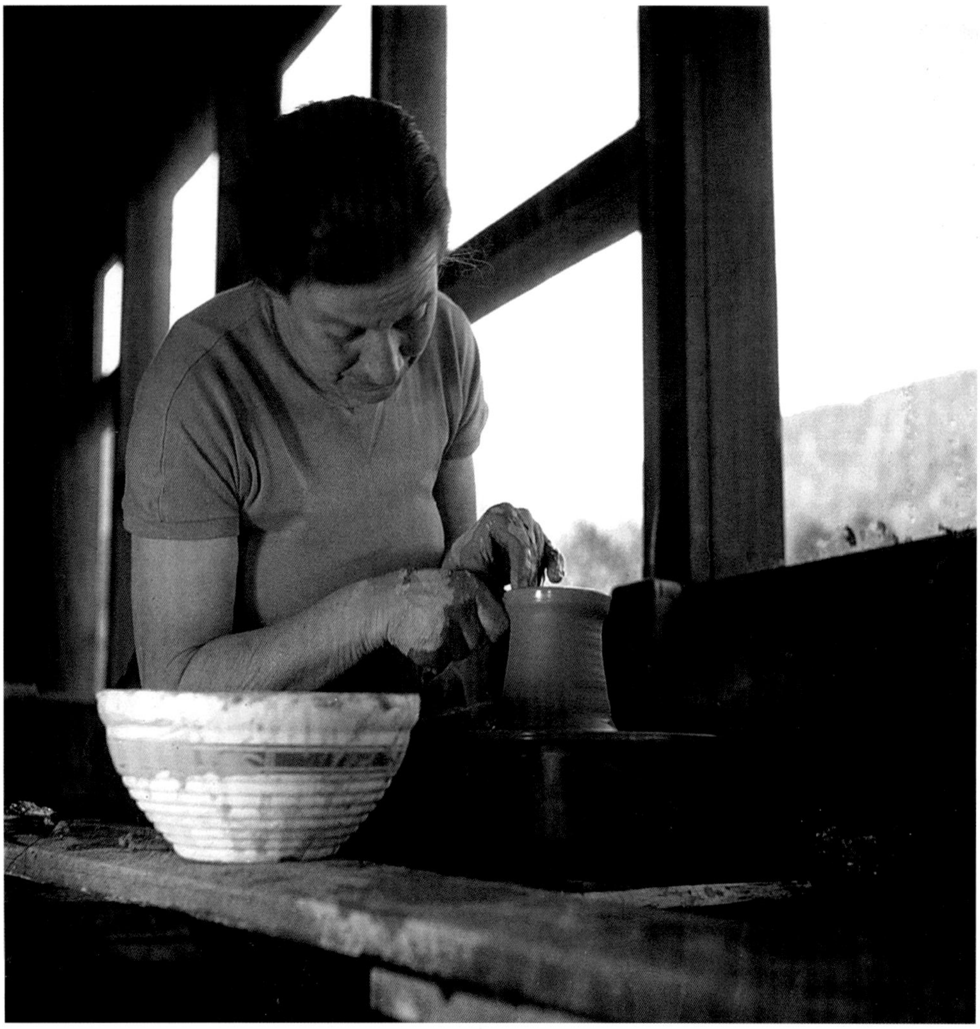

Marguerite Wildenhain, 1952

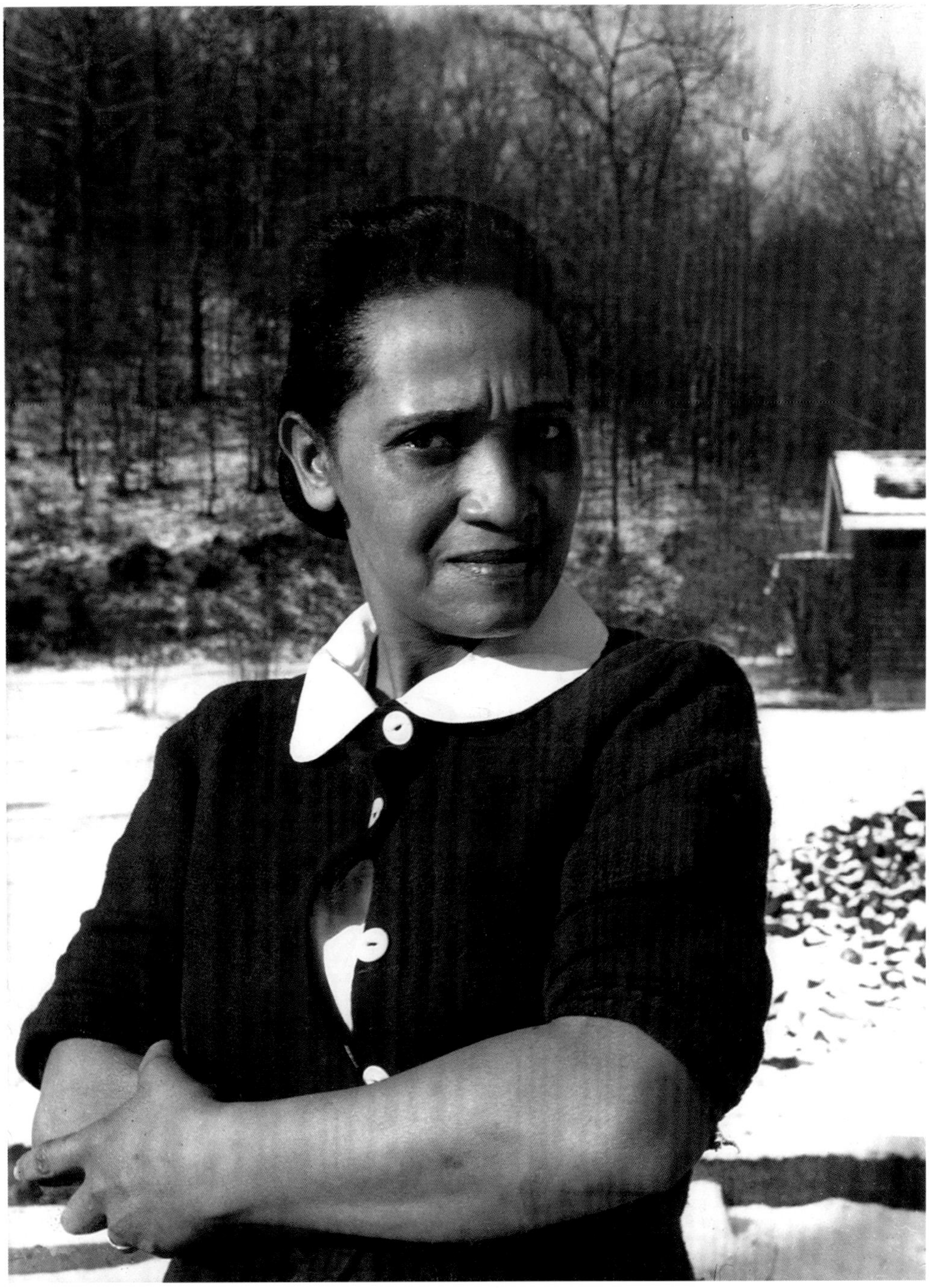

Cornelia Williams

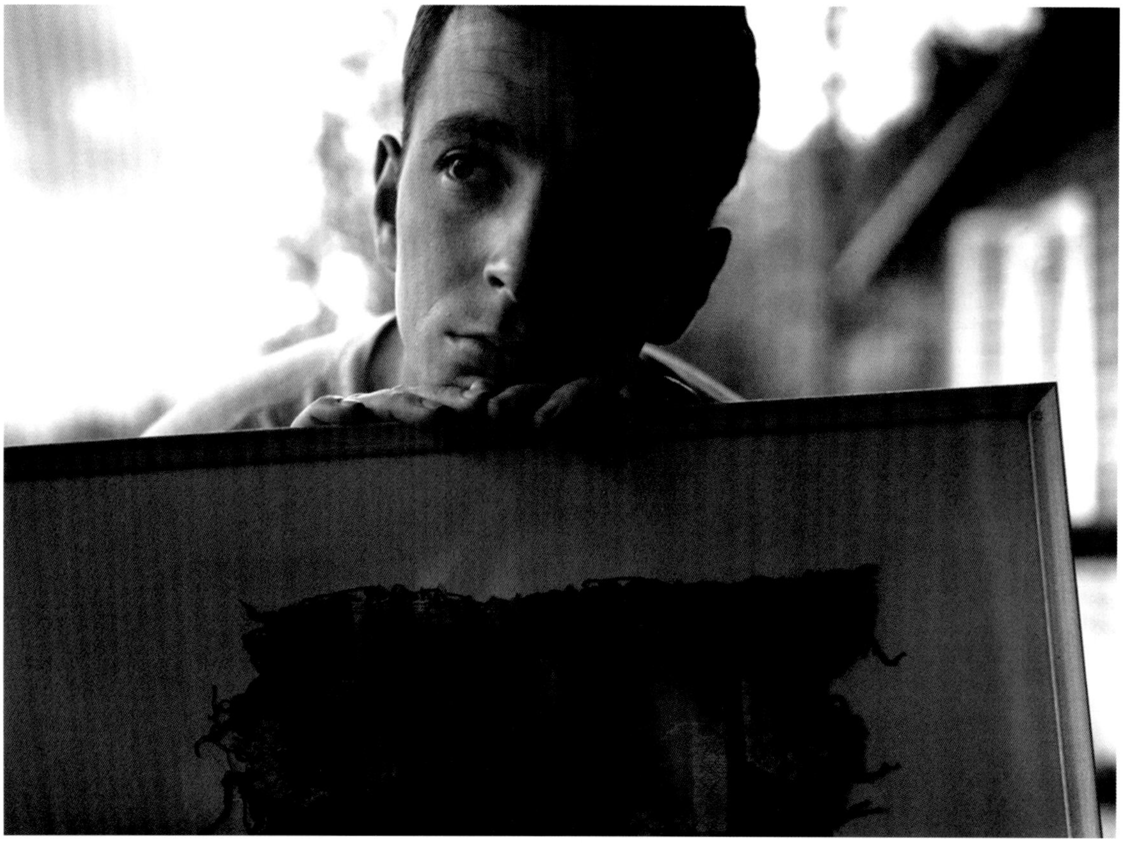

BMC student with a piece from the Engelhardt Textile Collection

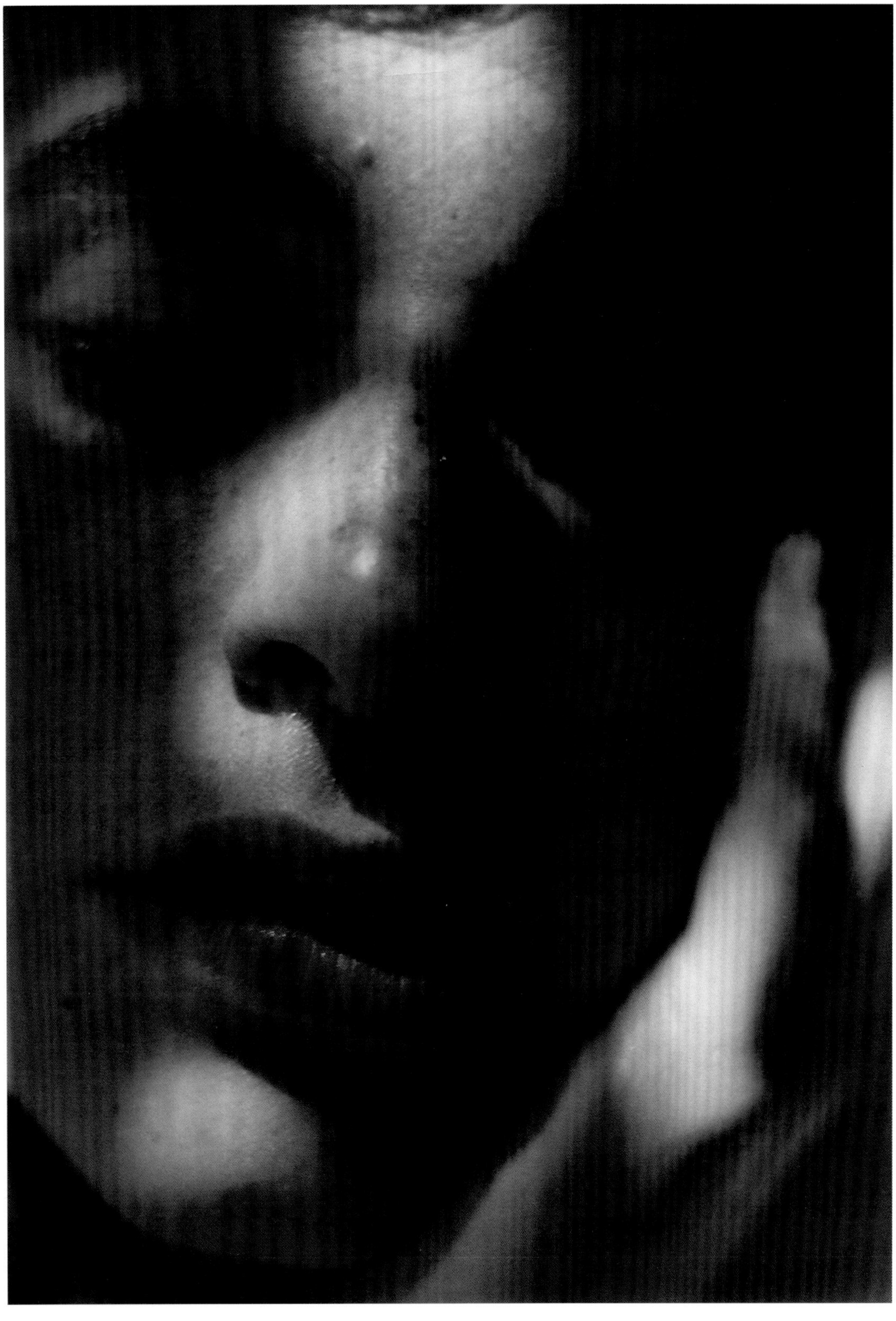

Untitled

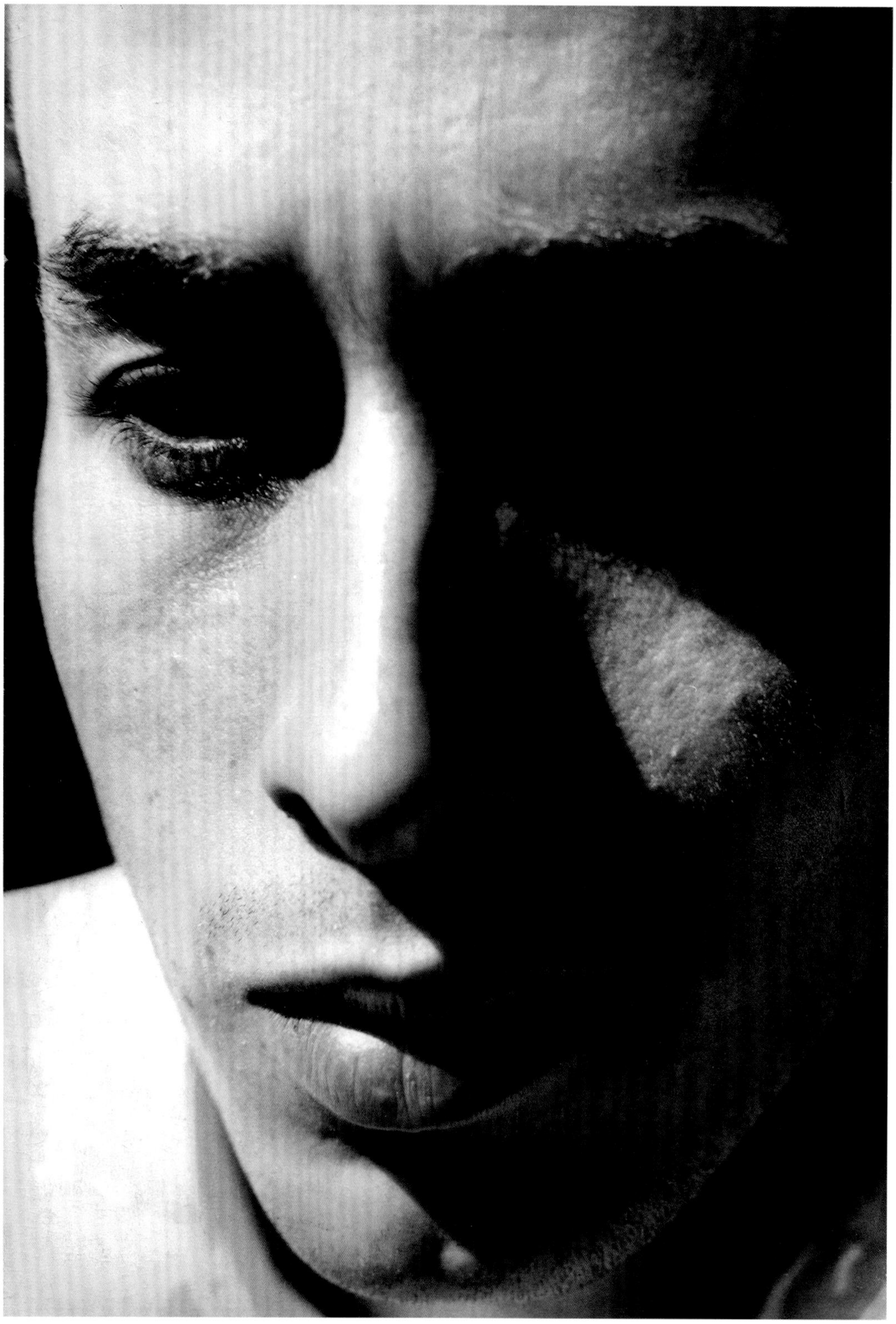

Untitled

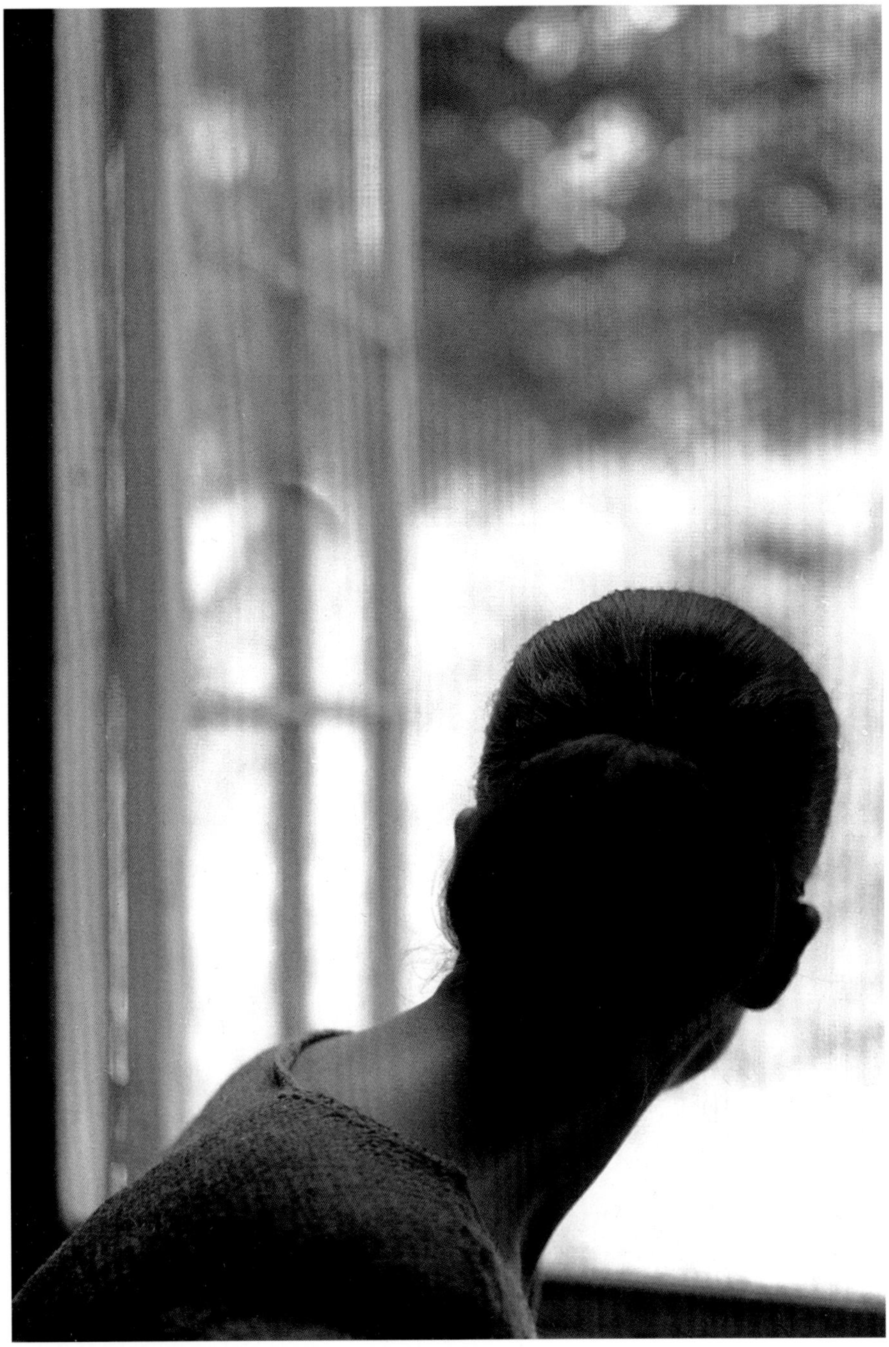

Untitled

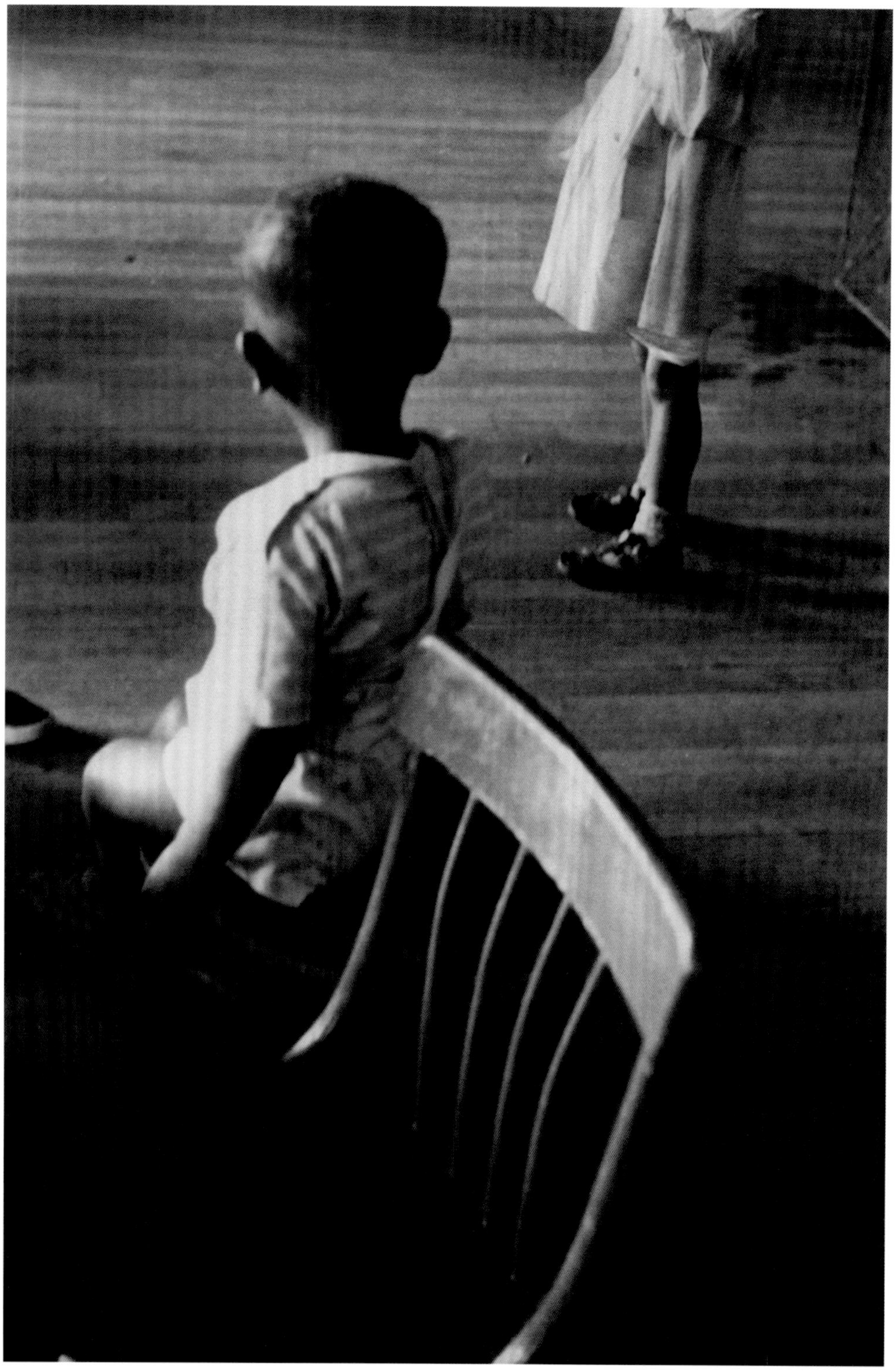

Untitled

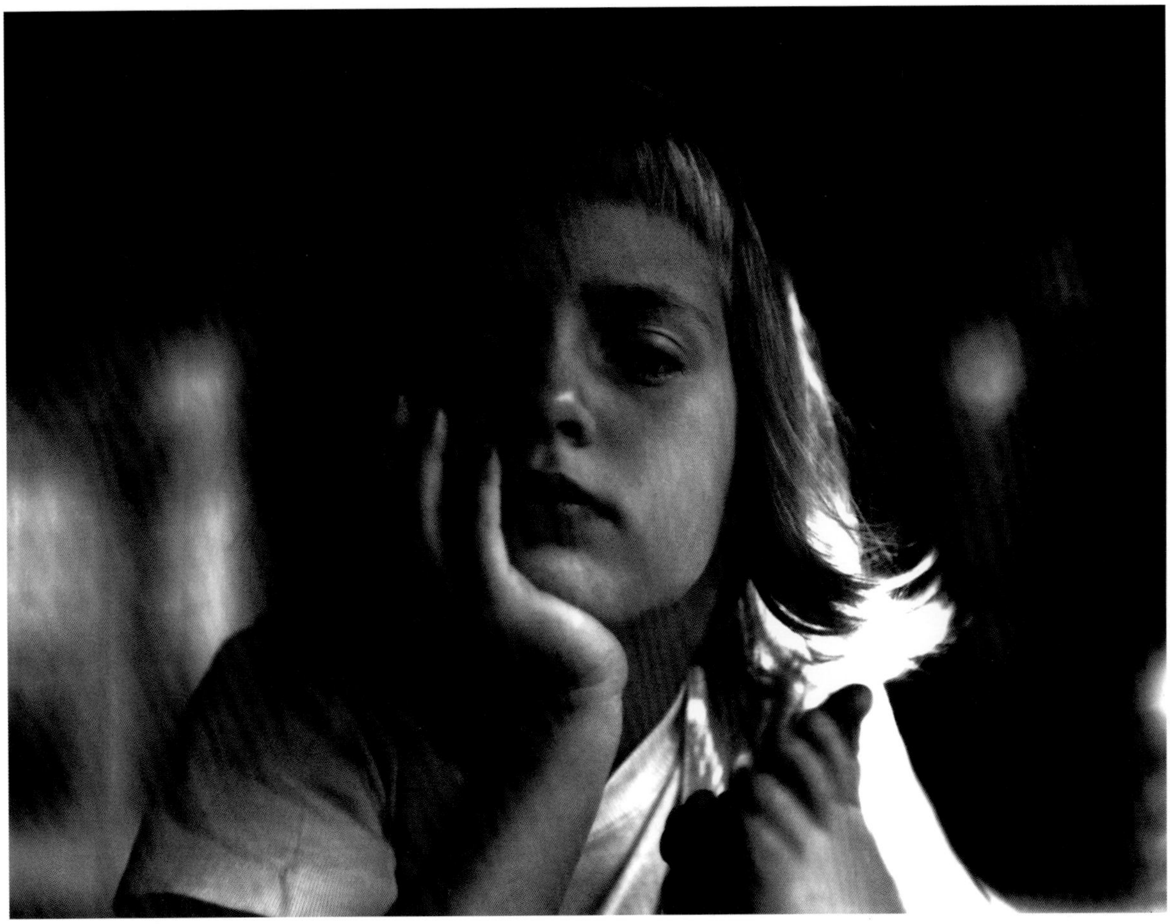

Untitled

# NATURE

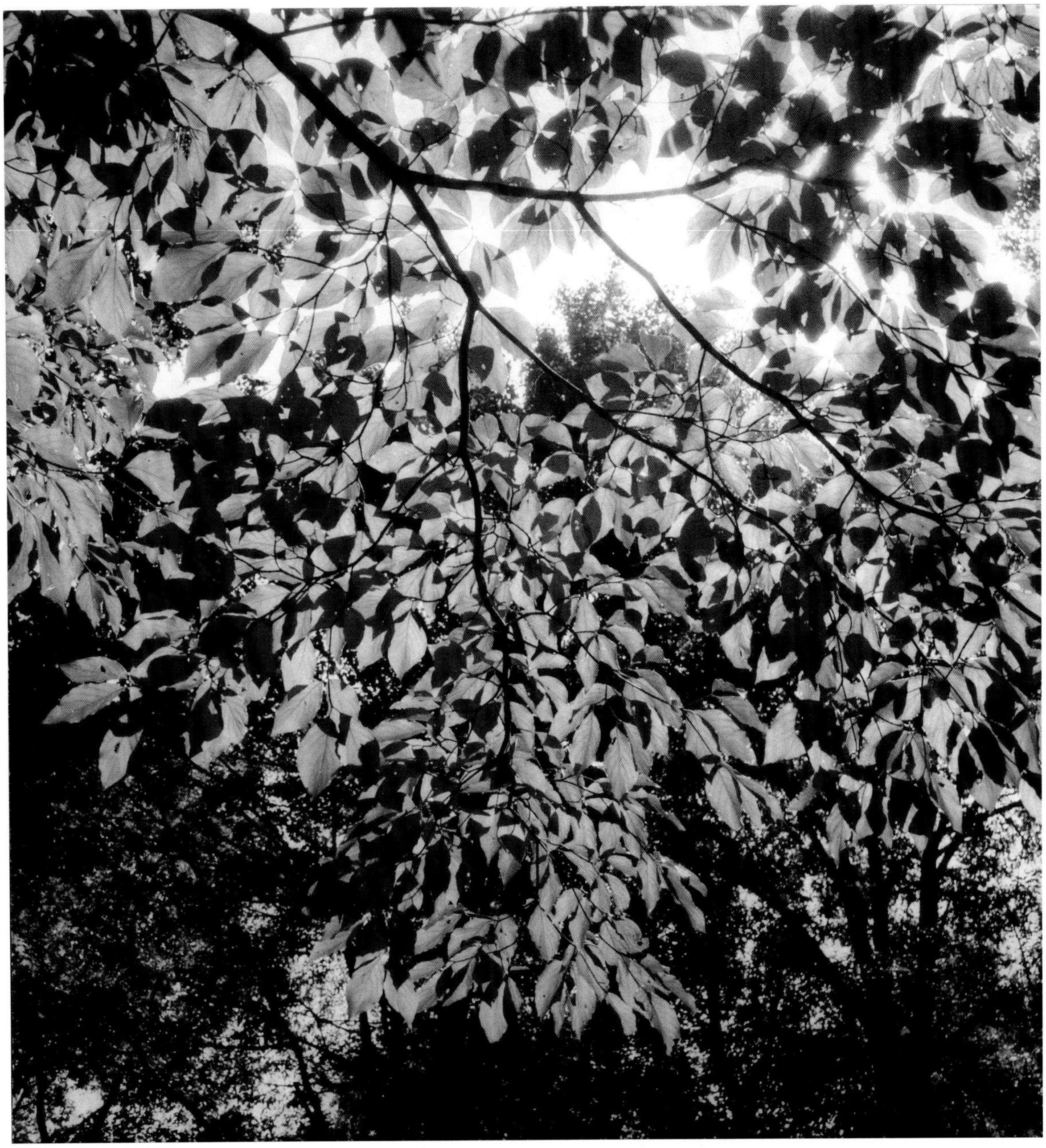

Untitled

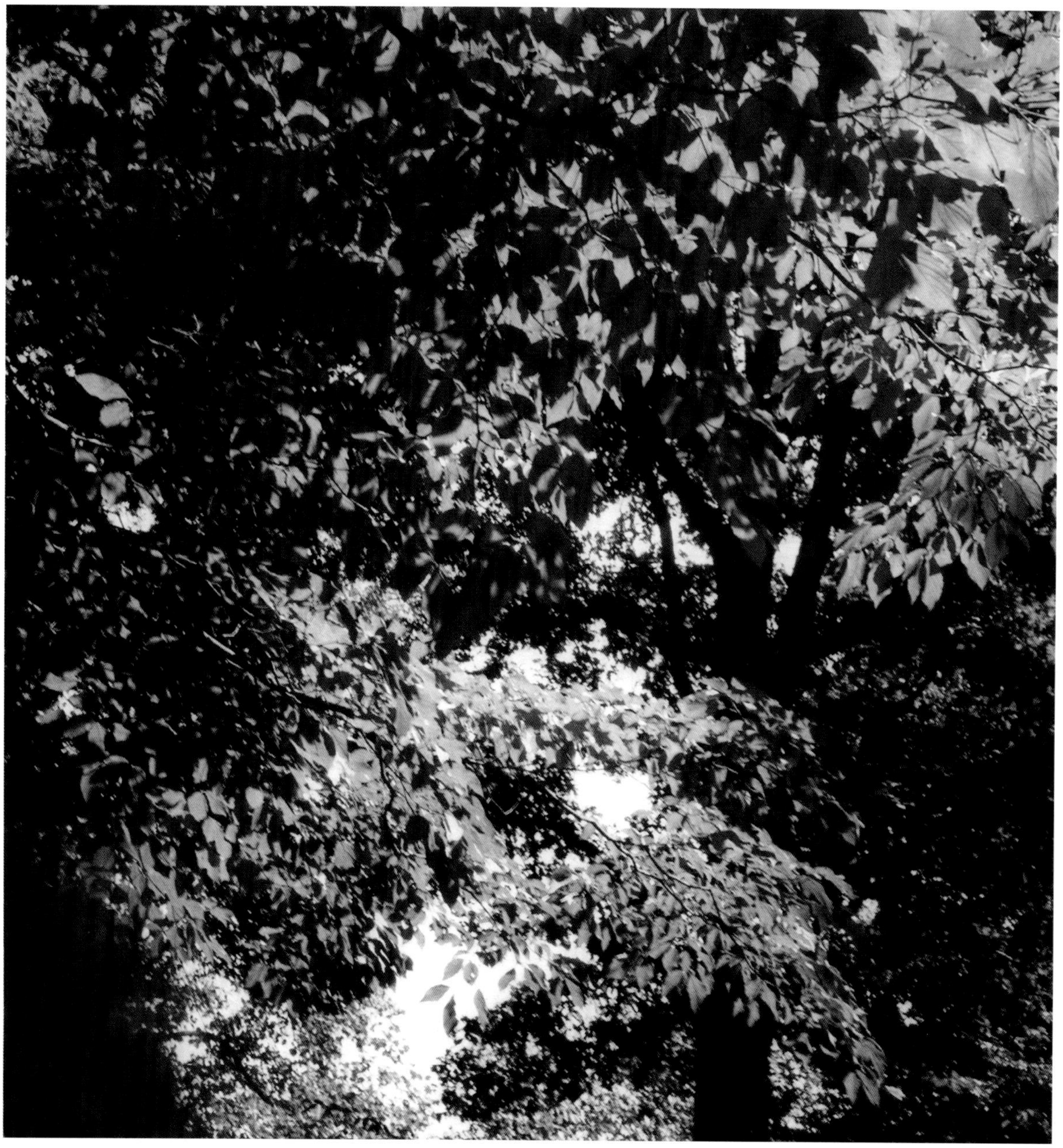

Untitled

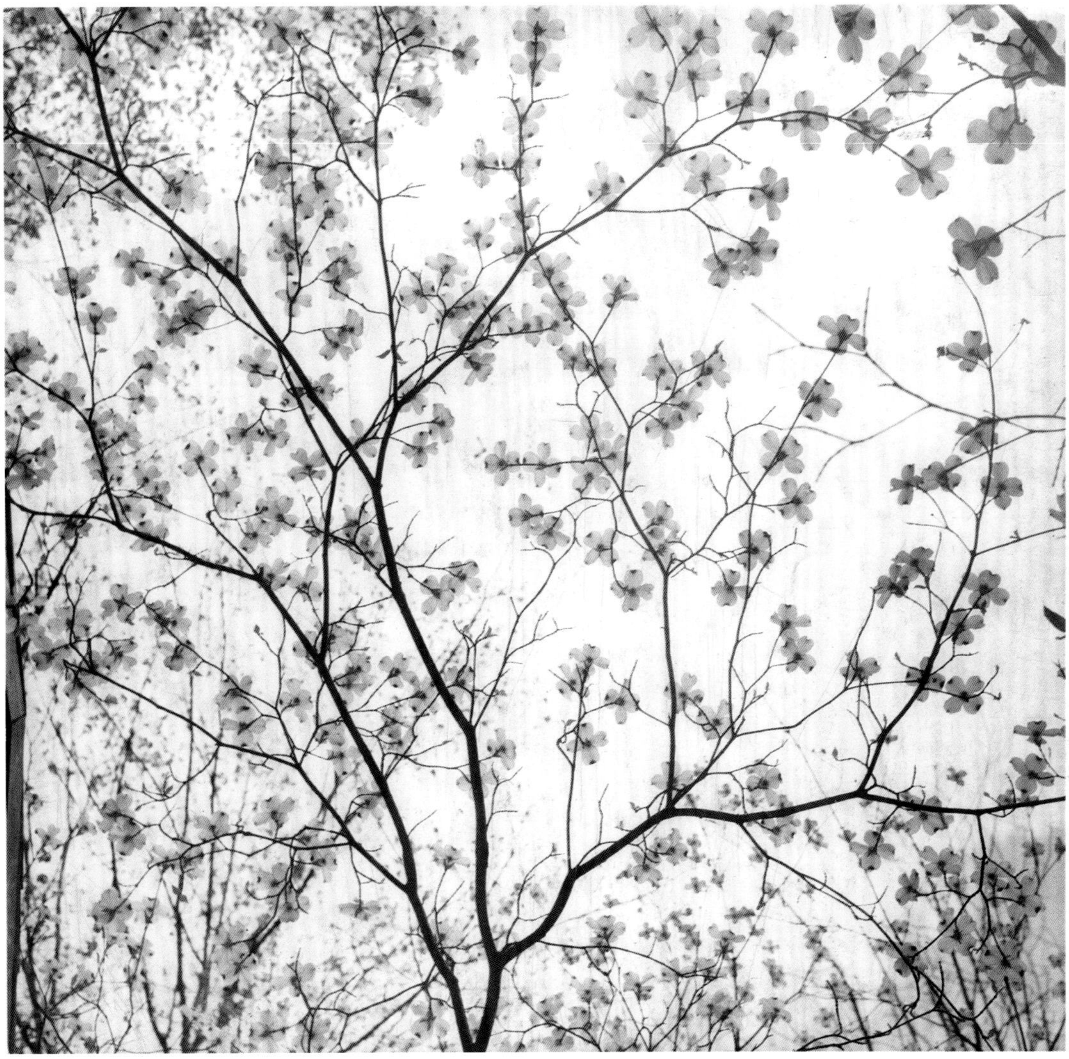

Dogwood Blossoms

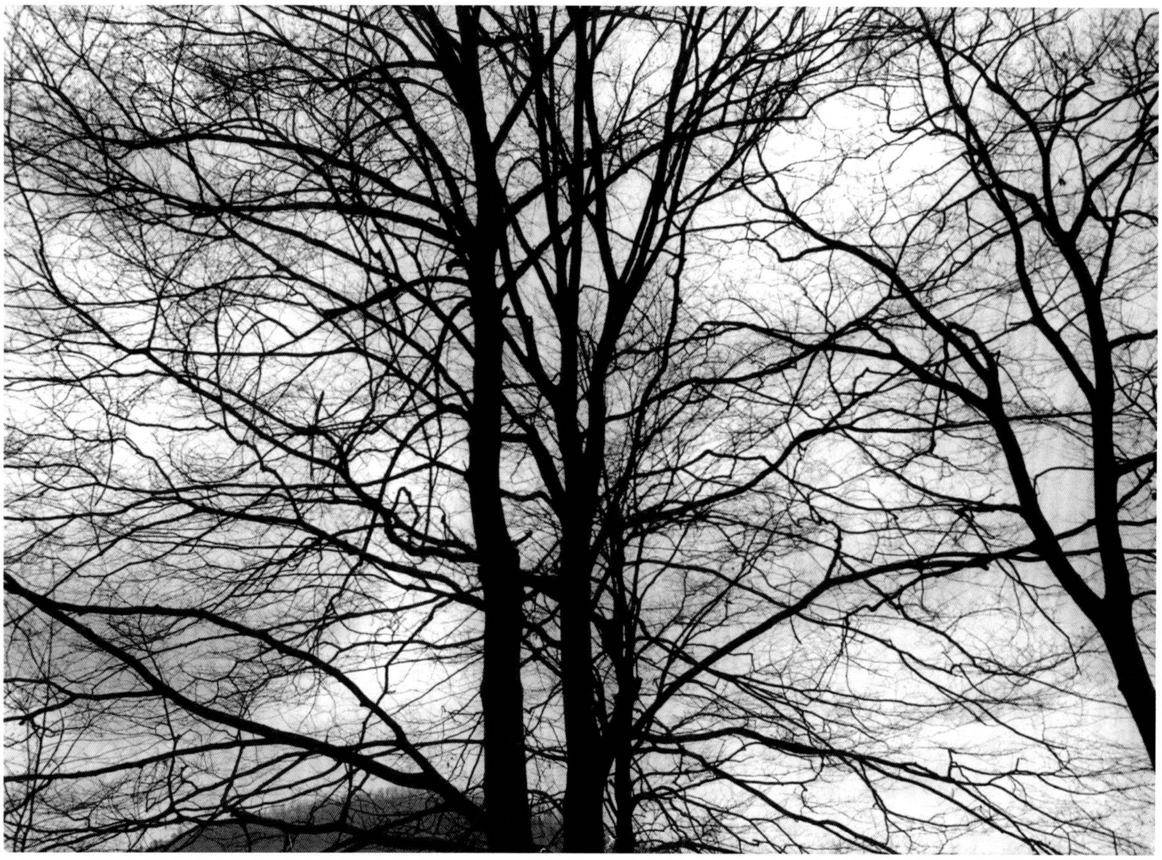

Untitled

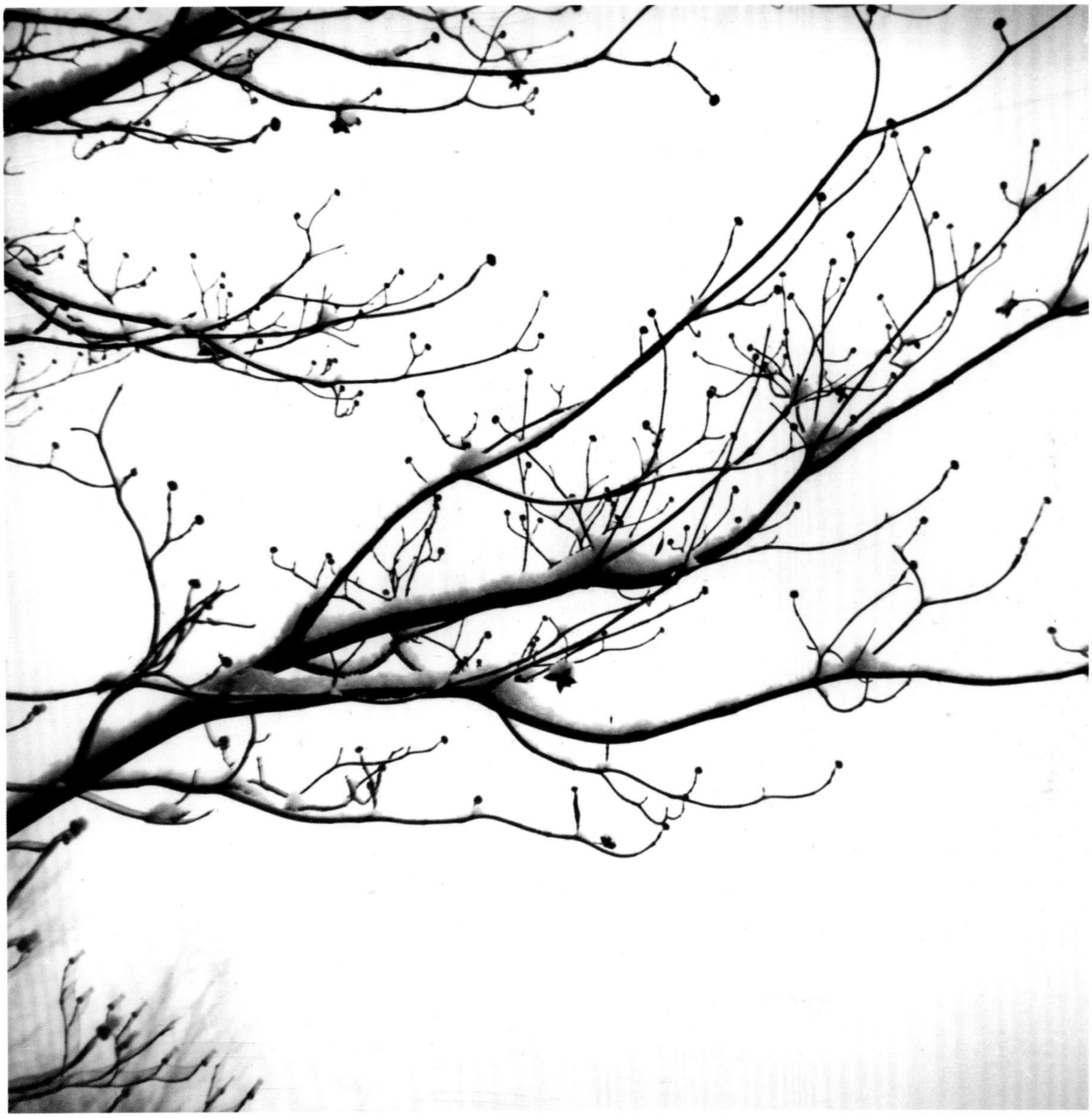

Untitled

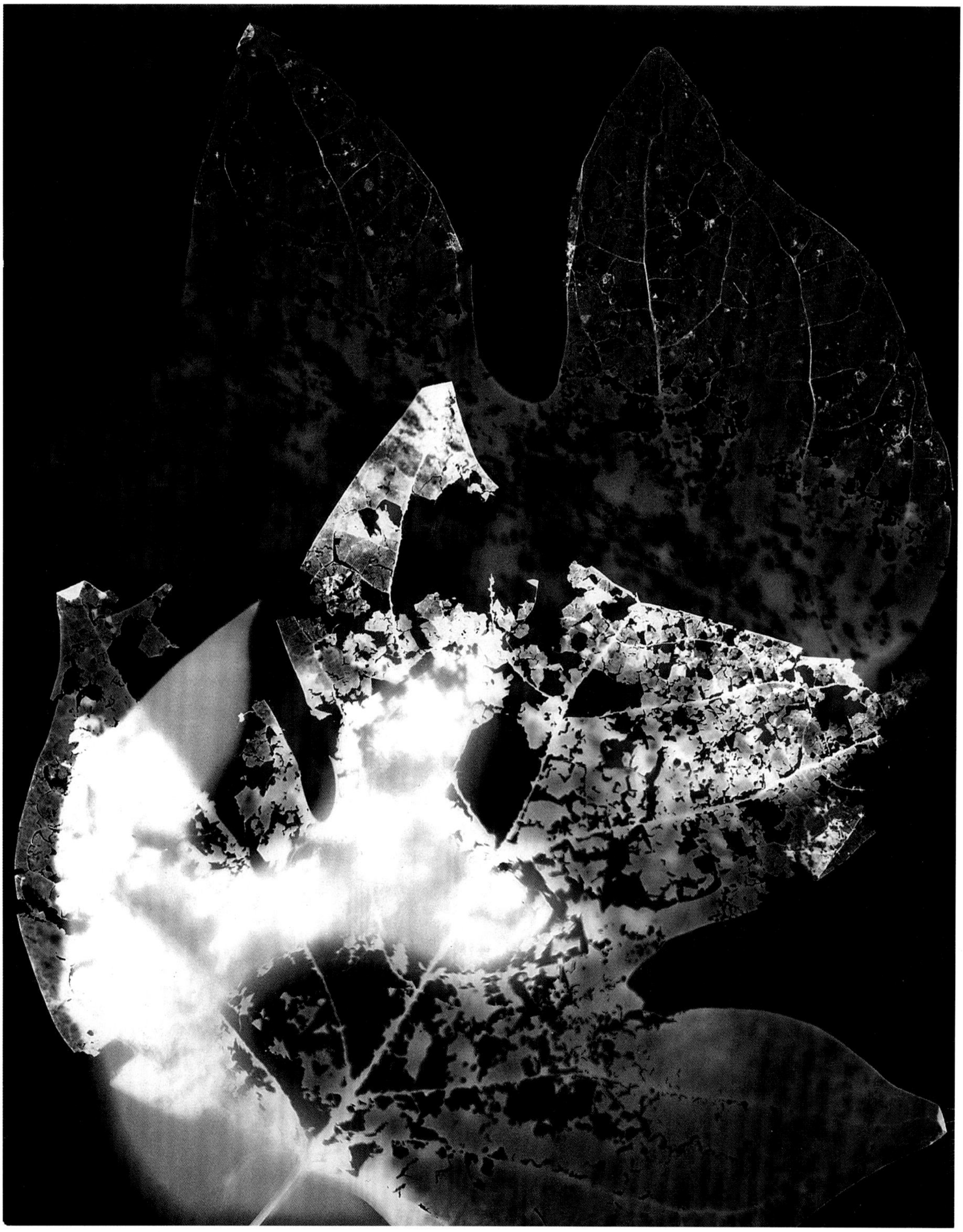

Untitled (Photogram)

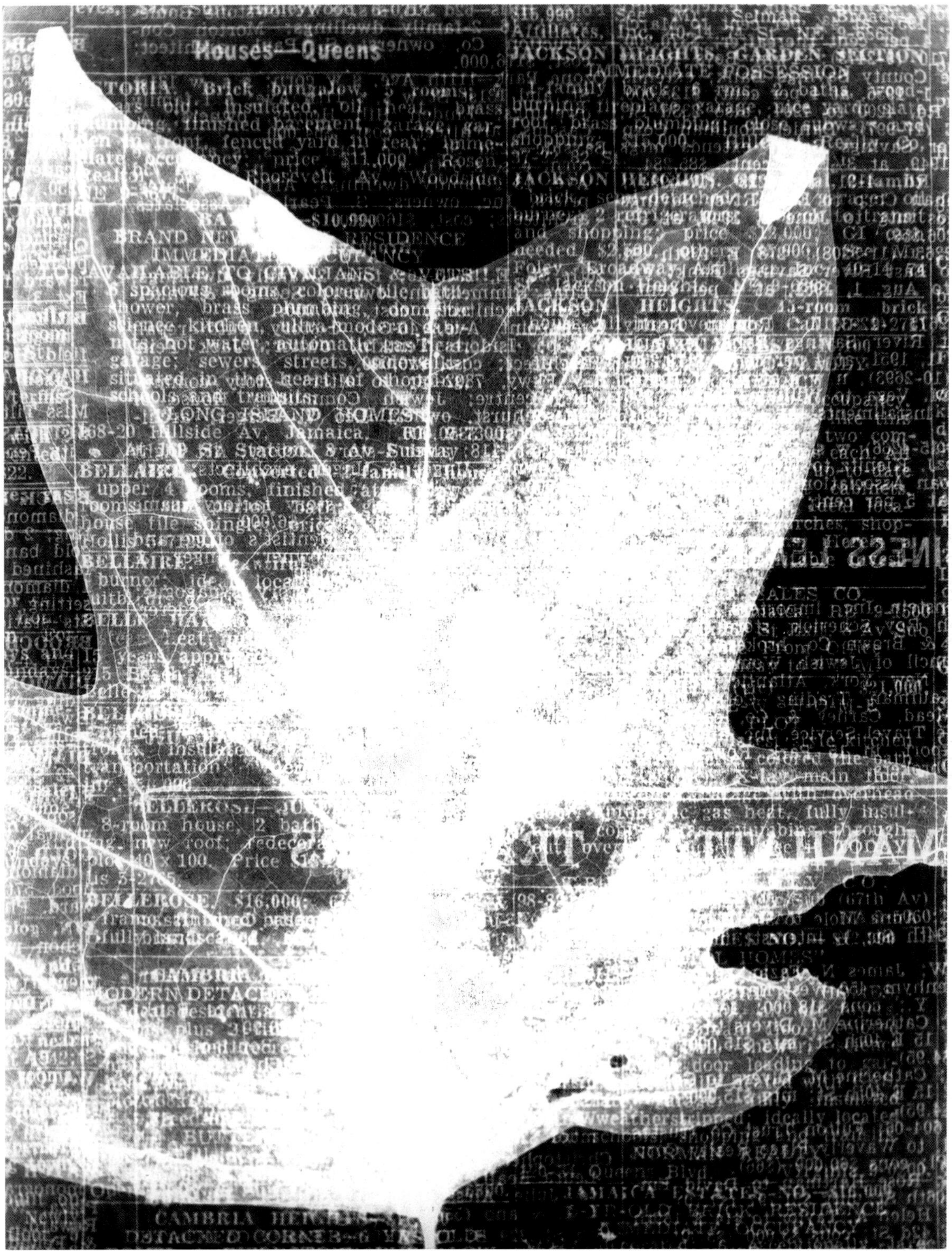


Untitled (Photogram)

## JOHN SIMON GUGGENHEIM MEMORIAL FOUNDATION

### Confidential Report on Candidate for Fellowship

Have known Hazel-Frieda Larsen Archer and her work since 1948. Her extraordinary vision of the life experience and genius in communicating it by means of the camera and dark room physiochemistry may be Emersonian "Compensation" or spontaneous genius, effective despite almost insurmountable handicaps.

At Black Mountain College, where I visited as a lecturer in 1948, the administration had admitted her as a special scholarship case. Students were sensitive to her delicate sensitivity and loved her and cared for her. Some one by intuition and generosity gave her a camera and fortunately a good versatile Rolleiflex.

Hazel began then to communicate spontaneously what she saw as she sat so long and quietly. She saw what we who hurry never have the time to see. She saw the life processes. She saw the tree photo-converting the sun radiation; she saw the tree breathing — She saw the ages processing beautifully and inexorably as she photographed the same side of a barn moment by moment and hour by hour; and she let us see with her what we had never been privileged to see before.

As she watched and sensed and thought and communicated the vision, out of phase to most of us, her soul seemed to expand and she began to communicate quietly in spoken words as well, and she listened intently to others' thoughts, and in fact, seemed to see them think. She took pictures of me at work with my mathematical structures and I know that she saw me thinking and what I was thinking about that the pictures made people understand what I had been unable myself to tell them about my structures and their mathematical significance. And those who danced knew that she had seen in their dance and made visible to others that which their dance had been unable to communicate directly.

Soon we knew that Hazel had a true genius, and one so subtle that in the rush and shock sequences of our moment in evolution would in its purity and simplicity be invisible for a while — so does nature protect her important new tendrilling. — But as I for one reopen those back pages of the file and accidentally turn up one of Hazel's pictures, I feel a sense of spontaneous delight and increased confidence in the overall integrity of life and universe clearly pulsing serenely in her photographs which unlike yesterday's news pictures seem to be eternally young and sustaining news.

I hesitate to write this letter on her behalf. As Mr. Moe could tell you, I have been writing my supporting thoughts regarding your candidates annually for a quarter of a century (only upon your request, and only for what I consider to be justifying circumstances) and none of those applicants have been successful in winning one of your fellowships.

I had resolved to withdraw my support as apparently unfortunate but feel that I would be traitorous in this instance were I to fail to restate my estimate of this applicant who asked and received my unreserved endorsement several years ago.

R. Buckminster Fuller
November 2, 1955

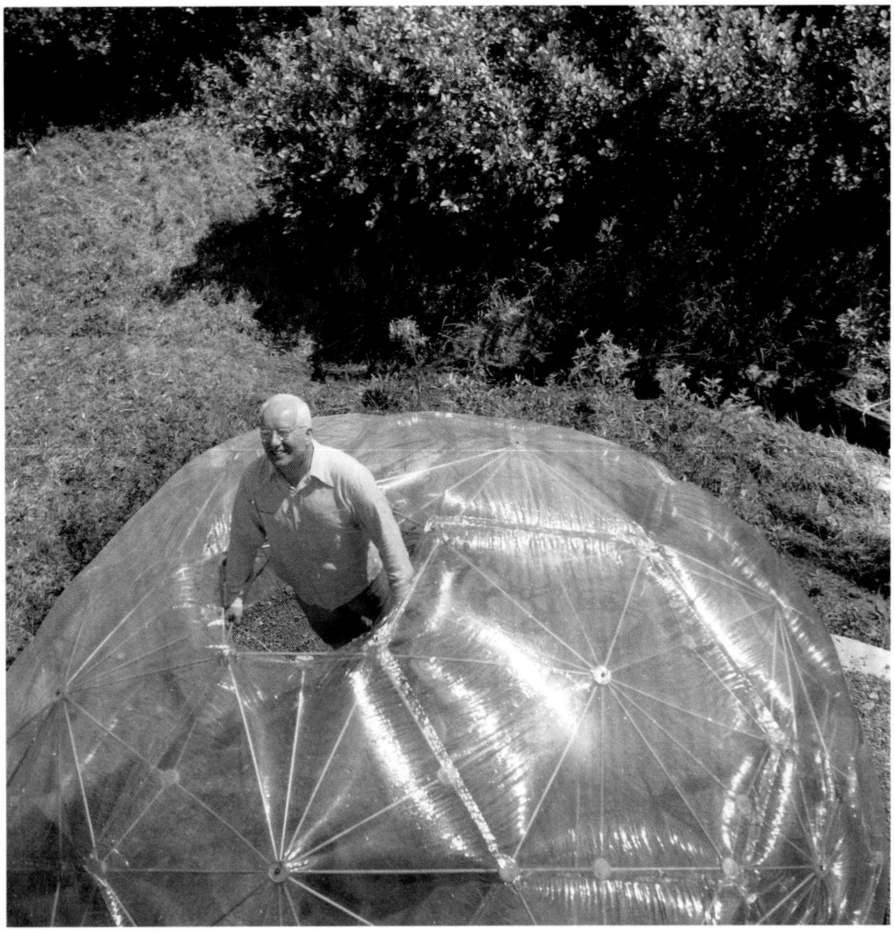

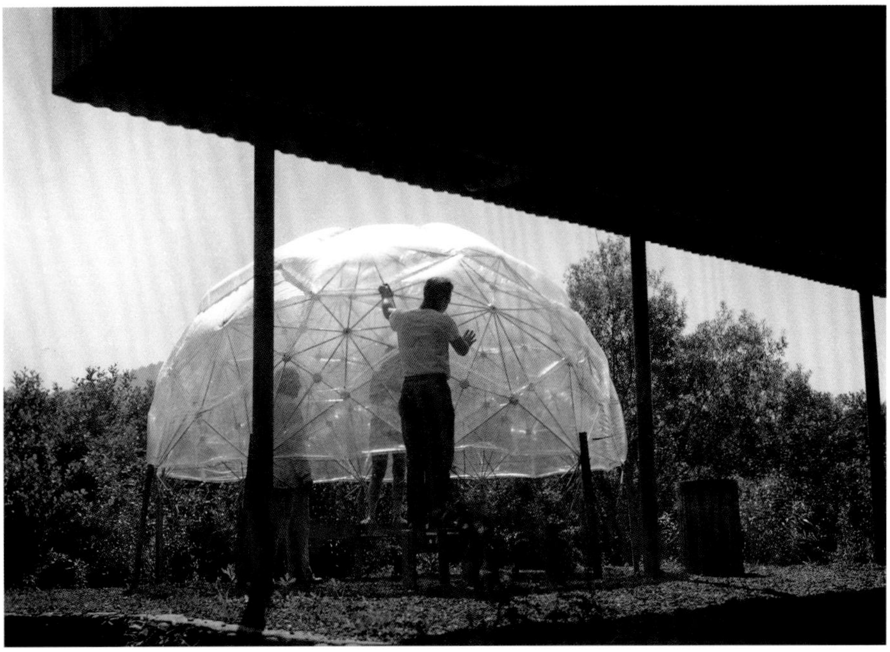

Buckminster Fuller

Buckminster Fuller with students and Geodesic Dome, Summer 1949

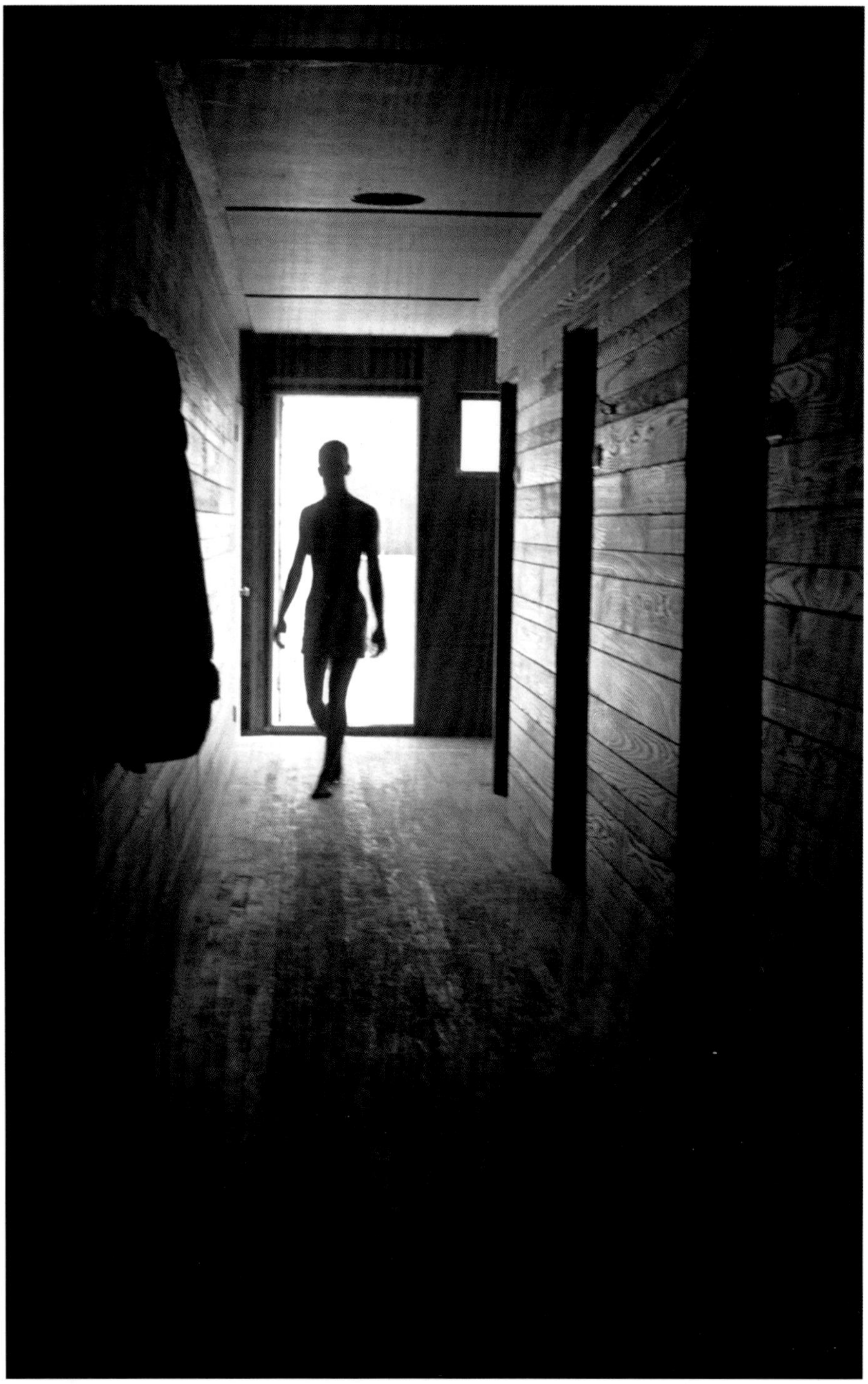

Ray Johnson in the Studies Building